MAKE SMART CHOICES

Learn How to Think Clearly, Beat Information Anxiety, Improve Decision Making Skills, and Solve Problems Faster

Som Bathla

www.sombathla.com

Table of Contents

Your Free Gift 6
Introduction 7
   Every Moment is a Moment of Choice 9
   You Still Make Decisions Even If You Think You Don't 11
   What You'll Learn in This Book 14
Chapter 1: Why Do Most People Struggle with Decision Making? 16
   What is Decision Making? 16
   2 Most Common Challenges 18
   Additional Challenges When Stakes Are High 22
Chapter 2: Why do You End up Making Bad Choices? 28
   Anchoring Trap 29
   Status Quo Trap 30
   Confirming Evidence Trap 33
   Framing Trap 35
   Recallability Trap 36
Chapter 3: Understand and Improve Your Decision-Maker Archetype 41

Maximizer 42

Satisficer 44

Perfectionist 46

Optimalist 47

Chapter 4: Effective Techniques to Eradicate Erroneous Thinking 52

Unconscious Associations Trigger Wrong Decisions 54

Avoid the Liking or Mirroring bias -- Stop Being Manipulated 57

Use the Observers Perspective for Objective Decisions 60

Shift Autopilot behavior to Manual Behavior 61

Change Behavior with Deadlines or Partitions 63

Chapter 5: Why You Don't Always Need More Information? 68

Don't Always Decide in Yes or No 69

Multi-tracking of Information 72

Avoid Choice Overload 75

Avoid Irrelevant Information 77

Follow the 40:70 Rule 81

Chapter 6: A Proactive Smart Choice Approach+ Using Ancient Intelligence (AI) 87

The PrOACT Approach 89

Use Ancient Intelligence to Autopilot your decisions... 96

Chapter 7: How to Find Solutions Quickly around You.. 104

Solution Finders are Givers 105

Gain from Your Competitors 107

Don't Ignore the Outside View -- Use Base Rates 109

Avoid Important Decisions in Stress Mode 113

Experiment New Ideas with Ooching 114

Chapter 8: 4 Simple Steps to Make Holistic Decisions 120

How to Make Holistic Decisions 120

Widen Your Alternatives 122

Reality-test your Assumptions 125

Attain Distance 129

Prepare to be Wrong 131

Chapter 9: How to Approach Your Future as your Most Trusted Guide 137

Follow the 10/10/10 Rule 139

Use Prospective Hindsight 141

Final Thoughts 147

May I ask you for a small favor? 149

Full Book Summary 151

Preview of the book "Build a Happier Brain" 175
Other Books in Power-Up Your Brain Series 188

Your Free Gift

As a token of my thanks for taking time to read my book, I would like to offer you a free gift:

Click below and download your **Free Report**

Learn 5 Mental Shifts to Turbo-Charge Your Performance in Every Area of Your Life - in the Next 30 Days!

You can also grab your FREE GIFT report through the below URL:

https://sombathla.lpages.co/5mentalshifts_msc/

Introduction

****

> *"Success emerges from the quality of the decisions we make and the quantity of luck we receive. We can't control luck. But we can control the way we make choices."*
>
> *— Chip Heath*

A group of children are playing near two different railway tracks.

While one track is operational, the other is disused. Only one child is on the disused track, and the rest of the children are playing on the operational track.

A passenger train is approaching fast.

In this situation, assume you are just standing beside the track interchange. You are in control of the track and can change the track whatever way you decide. Since, you are standing quite far from the children, you don't have enough time to go or shout to the kids about a fast approaching train.

You have two choices here.

You can make the train change its course to the disused track and save most of the kids by sacrificing the life of a lone child playing on the disused track. Or would you rather let the train go on its way?

Most people would choose diverting the course of the train and sacrifice only one child to save the lives of ten children.

One life versus ten – ten lives are more precious. Seems an obvious decision, doesn't it?

When I heard this the first time, I instantly thought this way only because saving the lives of many children by sacrificing life of one child appears to be a rational decision that most people would make, morally and emotionally.

But pause for a moment and think a bit harder. What is the fault of the child choosing to play on the disused track, who in fact made a right decision to play in a safe place?

Why does his life warrant a sacrifice merely because his ignorant friends chose to play where the danger was?

Leo Velski Julian, a critic who told the above story, said he would not try to change the course of the train because he believed that the kids playing on the operational track should have known very well that the track was still in use, and they should have run away when they heard the train's siren.

If the train had been diverted, that lone child would definitely die because he never thought the train would come over to that track. Moreover, that track was not in use probably because it was not safe. If the train had been diverted to the track, the lives of all passengers on board would have been at stake. And in your attempt to save a few kids by sacrificing one child, you might end up sacrificing hundreds of people.

You might have realized by now how a decision that immediately seemed like a straight forward choice (though emotionally a bit hard) can prove to be a worse choice, with a little bit of thinking.

Life sometimes offers tough choices in disguised form, and making hasty decisions in such situations may not always be the right move.

Though all the decisions in front of us are not of life or death situations, still there is no denying that we have to make decisions almost all the time.

Every Moment is a Moment of Choice

Every day and every moment, we have to make some kind of decision: they add up. They could be miniature choices with minimal impact, or they could be big decisions that can change the trajectory of your life.

A few examples of simple and low (or no) impact choices could be:

- What to eat, which restaurant to visit, or what cuisine/dish to order?
- What to wear to your office or a party today?
- What route to take to the office if you are late, so you don't get into heavy traffic?
- Which movie to watch this weekend, with whom to go, and what theatre?
- Whether to go out for drinks with friends or have a fun evening with the kids?

You see that the above decisions are really simple decisions, and the difference is just some moments of pleasure if you make them right, or a sad evening, if you don't choose correcting.

But there are times when life requires you to take a leap forward and make huge decisions like:

- What career to opt for or which college/university to enter?
- What companies to apply to for jobs?

- Whether to continue in the same job, change jobs, or make an altogether career move and explore new ways to reach your dreams.
- Should you marry now or wait 3-4 years? What kind of life partner to the tie knot with?
- If you get married, do you want to have kids now or in a few years?

The above questions are difficult, life-altering decisions with high stakes, and the consequences will keep tormenting you for years if you don't make the right choices.

You see, all decisions are not equal, so they don't pose an equal level of challenge. Some decisions take less energy and others take lot of time, effort, and even cause a lot of stress. Any decision becomes easy or difficult depending on the stakes involved. Choosing a food item from a menu is easier than finding employment in a new sector or starting a business venture.

The bottom line is that the nature of problems may vary, but you have to make decisions -- small decisions and big decisions every time.

Therefore, it wouldn't be incorrect to say: You don't have a choice except to make a choice.

You Still Make Decisions Even If You Think You Don't

There's one intriguing approach a few people follow. They think if they don't make any decisions, they will remain safe from the risks involved and the consequences that can arise.

But here is the thing.

Not making a decision is also a choice. Unconsciously, you might think you have not decided, but, in effect, you have chosen to ignore the situation, which in itself is a decision.

If you <u>don't wake up after your alarm goes off</u> and continue to stay in the bed, while you could hit the gym, you have unconsciously decided to choose laziness instead of fitness.

If you are <u>stuck in a job or are inadvertently trapped in a low-rewarding business</u> that no longer fascinates you, and you don't do anything about it, you've made a decision – a decision to let boredom, unhappiness and soon-to-be-highlighted issues of low performance emerge in your life.

If you <u>don't do anything and say you'll see and handle whatever happens in the future</u>, then you are choosing not to improve yourself per the changing demands of the environment, thus inviting in the troubles of becoming obsolete in the marketplace.

Yes, you made decisions in all the above cases, though you might erroneously think you haven't.

Take this famous real-world example of what happened to a huge corporation that chose not to make a decision.

Kodak was a pioneer in film-based photography. The giant was a market leader during times when cameras required inserting physical film to take pictures that later needed to be developed through a chemical process to generate a physical photograph. Unlike today's digital cameras, you had no way of knowing how they would look, until you saw the physically-developed prints.

Kodak continued to produce film-based cameras for decades and was ruling the industry. Despite the fact that *digital* photography was invented by a Kodak engineer, the management simply ignored it. During the later years of twentieth century, when digital photography was emerging, Kodak didn't pay the required attention to this new disruptive technology and all but missed the digital wave.

What was the result? New digital camera companies started enjoying dominance in the camera business, rising over Kodak, and it was not long before Kodak had to shut down its shops.

What was wrong with Kodak's approach?

Kodak just continued what it had been doing for years. It simply did not decide, and this non-decision proved to be the worst decision of Kodak.

In a nutshell, you have to make decisions every time, and if you don't decide, don't kid yourself, you have still made the decision not to make a decision.

Decision making, therefore, is one of the most important life skills.

What You'll Learn in This Book

My objective in writing this book is to empower you think better and make smarter decisions by developing the right mental framework and applying actionable strategies. This book will make you aware of your decision-making archetype based on the end objective behind any choices. You will learn about four different types of decision makers and what makes them decide so differently.

You'll learn the common struggles that most people face in making decision and come to know about the hidden traps that lead to bad choices. It's only when you become aware of these traps or obstacles that you start making changes in your approach, because awareness is the very first step in any kind of transformation. Until you realize what is bad, you really don't have any motivation to change yourself.

This book is loaded with scientific and psychological research to help you overcome your thinking biases or erroneous beliefs and equip yourself with new tools and parameters to decide more intelligently and make better and more decisions in less time.

Now, without further ado, let's move to Chapter 1 and learn about the most common reasons why people struggle with making decisions.

Introduction- Key Takeaways

Every moment of your life requires you to make some kind of decision. It could be a small miniature choice or a life-altering decision.

Even if you don't decide on any particular situation, you unconsciously made a choice to not decide on that matter.

Not doing anything and just waiting to see what happens in the future is nothing but a decision to not improve and adapt yourself to today's dynamic and ever-changing world, thus becoming obsolete and easily replaceable by those who consistently change.

Chapter 1: Why Do Most People Struggle with Decision Making?

****

> *"Inability to make decisions is one of the principal reasons executives fail. Deficiency in decision-making ranks much higher than lack of specific knowledge or technical know-how."*
>
> *~John C. Maxwell*

In the brief introduction, you already learned how decision making is all pervasive and plays a vital role in creating an optimal life. In this section, we'll start with the fundamentals – let's understand what decision making really is and then learn the key challenges in making decisions.

What is Decision Making?

The Latin meaning of the word

"decision" is "to cut off." Making a decision is about "cutting off" choices — cutting off other courses of actions and come out with a final choice among many.

Decision making is, in fact, a mental or cognitive process that results in the selection of a course of action among several alternative possibilities. It is a process of identifying and choosing the best alternative based on the values, preferences, and beliefs of the decision maker.

Although the definition is straightforward, i.e., choosing one alternative out of many, but the hard reality comes in when there are multiple parameters to look at to reach an end objective, including the expectations of different stakeholders, uncertainties, uncontrollable events, etc. - all of which require due consideration.

The number of parameters and the degree of the stake involved in the decision-making process make any decision either a simple or a difficult one. The more complexity involved and the higher the stake, the harder it is to make a decision!

Some people take lot of time and still get confused when deciding on cuisine at a restaurant or selecting a daily outfit. They get overwhelmed with such minute dining choices when offered a range of alternative.

On the other hand, you might have seen people who make high-level difficult decisions without a flinch. All the time, business leaders make big decisions like launching a new product in the market, setting up a new profitable venture despite cut-throat competition, or convincing investors to raise more funds; and the list goes on and on. All these decisions require taking into account multiple parameters, a complex market environment and the needs of demanding stakeholders. You can imagine the heightened level of decision-making skill such people have developed.

We will cover in detail the strategies and tools high-achievers have in their toolbox to make better, smarter, and faster decisions in later chapters. But for now, let's try to **understand why the majority of people struggle and the nature of their key challenges in making decisions**. Here are a few factors that lead to making bad decisions, procrastinating or not making a decision at all.

2 Most Common Challenges

Information Overload

People are too obsessed with collecting more and more information for making their decisions. Also referred to as **infoxication or infobesity**, this situation is where you collect so much information in your head that you're unable to cohesively organize and process it to arrive at any decision.

Psychologist George Miller of Princeton University presented a paper in psychology, stating that the human brain can process about **seven (+/- two) chunks of information** at a time (also known as Miller's Law). Miller says that under overload conditions, people become confused and are likely to make poor decisions based on the information they have received, as opposed to making informed ones.

Information overload occurs when the amount of input to your brain's cognitive faculties exceeds its processing capacity. Since you are flooded with information, you are unable to properly analyze it due to a shortage of time, resources or your cognitive bandwidth; therefore, you end up making poor quality decisions.

Clay Shirky, a writer, consultant and professor at New York University on the social and economic effects of Internet technologies and journalism, states that information overload in the modern age is a consequence of a deeper problem that he calls *filter failure*.

Let's see what happens in the case of filter failure.

When filters fail, you are confronted by things you have no interest in and spam starts to enter your primary inbox. In other words, **you are**

not able to filter what is relevant and important, what you should consume, or how new information should come to you.

The advent of information technology has been the key driver in augmenting information overload for multiple reasons. You are exposed to massive amounts of information, given the ease of dissemination, and also people have enhanced their ability to spread that information outreach due to the vast output of social media, paid advertising, etc.

Finally, with too much information occupying the limited space in our heads, it becomes difficult to properly analyze a situation and make a decision.

Paralysis by Analysis

The next bigger challenge in making decisions is paralysis by analysis.

Paralysis by analysis is a state of over-thinking and analyzing a particular problem for an unreasonably long time and still end up not making a decision. Here you find yourself paralyzed in making any kind of moves, because an overdose of thinking has crippled your ability to choose a particular direction.

In the information overload situation (as discussed above), you get exposed to too much of information and you find yourself grappling with the sheer volume of it; and that in itself overwhelms you. However, in the case of paralysis by analysis, you keep on analyzing loads and loads of information, and due to this, you start finding some fault with every alternative and fail to zero down on a single alternative.

The ancient short fable of the fox and the cat explains the situation of paralysis by analysis in a simple way.

In a jungle, a fox and a cat were discussing how many ways each of them have to escape, if they are chased by hunters. The fox boasts of having many alternatives. The cat, however, admits to having only one. When the hunters finally arrive, the cat quickly climbs a tree. The fox, on the other hand, begins to analyze all the ways he knows to escape from them. But unable to decide which one would be best, he fails to act and gets caught by their dogs.

This story does nothing but simply illustrate the analysis paralysis phenomenon: the inability to act or decide due to over-thinking about various available alternatives and possible outcomes.

Although they start with a good intention to find a solution to a problem, people often analyze indefinitely the various factors or parameters that might lead to wrong decisions.

Also, they don't feel satisfied with the available information and think they still need more data to perfect their decision. They keep on gathering more and more material, continue to interrogate more people, but, ironically, they are not able to decide anything.

Why do people take so much time and keep on overanalyzing a situation?

This often happens when someone is afraid of making a wrong decision that can lead to potential catastrophic consequences: it might impact their career or their organization's productivity, or even the overall objective of the bigger team. That's the reason why people are generally over-cautious in making decisions that involve huge stakes.

Additional Challenges When Stakes Are High

Apart from the challenges posed by excess of information, high-stake situations pose other and different kinds of challenges, as listed below:

Uncertainty

In complex decisions, a lot of facts are uncertain. If you are venturing into a new market, you don't know which will impact your launch and eventual profitability in a given market. Every uncertainty requires us to think about and make judgments of the different consequences that may arise, as well as the potential probability of each consequence.

While uncertainty carries with it new possibilities, hasty venturing into unknown territory poses a high risk. Therefore, uncertainty makes most people stay wherever they are currently and therefore end up not making decisions.

Complexity

In high-stake decision making, many interrelated factors need to be taken into account. You have to analyze the interrelationships between these factors and how each of them can be influenced by the others.

For example, when a town planner develops a new city or town, a huge number of factors require consideration. You have to plan, among other things, the availability of ground water, a sewerage system, building roads, and provisions for setting up an infrastructure to invite revenue-generation in the town. You can see that the sheer number of factors makes this highly complex. Plus, the complex interplay among various uncertain factors stresses people out when making decisions.

Important decisions like opting for a particular career or job, starting a new venture/launching a new product, looking for a perfect life partner, or finalizing the best higher education for your kid etc. are governed by interrelated factors, and how each of them interplays with the others can't be assessed with certainty, thus making such decisions complex.

The Consequences have a High-Stake Impact

When you realize that the consequences of erroneous decisions are really very high stake, it immediately slows down your decision-making process. You may think it is obvious that if the stakes are so high, then decisions need to be given more time to be analyzed before becoming final.

People tend to believe that spending more time pondering various alternatives, just because the stakes are high, and any errors would have costly implications puts them into a paralysis by analysis mode.

Too Many Alternatives

When you allow yourself to consider too many alternatives for a given problem, it vastly expands the scope of the decision making activity itself. Each alternative has different factors and uncertainties associated with it, and, therefore, its own set of pros and cons.

Comparing alternatives creates a huge web of complexity and, therefore, poses a big challenge to fast and effective decision making for many people. You'll understand later in the book about a concept of paradox of choice that explains the psychology behind why people are unable to make decisions when they are faced with so many alternatives.

Interpersonal issues

Last but not least, in the decision-making process, you need to take into account how other people respond to your decisions i.e., the reaction of all the stakeholders who get impacted. Meeting the expectations of different stakeholders and coming up with a decision that turns out to be a win-win proposition for everyone is definitely another level of challenge.

It's important to distinguish here that while the above challenges to decision making originate from the outside environment, there are many internal hidden traps that adversely affect an effective decision-making process and thus lead to bad decisions. In the next chapter, we will talk about some major pitfalls in our thinking patterns or belief systems – the hidden traps that trip us into making bad decisions.

Chapter 1- Key Takeaways

Making a decision is about "cutting off" choices — cutting off other courses of action and coming out with a final choice among many.

The two biggest challenges in decision making are:

1. **Information Overload**: As per Miller's Law, the human brain can process seven (+/- two) chunks of information at a time. But in today's information age, with the ease of information dissemination and vast outreach of social media, you are overexposed to information. This leads to **information overload because the amount of input to your brain's cognitive faculties far exceeds its processing capacity.**

Information overload also cause to "filter failure" for your brain, meaning you are unable to filter the relevant and important information from the irrelevant and insignificant details.

2. **Paralysis by Analysis**: This occurs when you start to overthink and overanalyze any situation and the available alternatives to resolve a given problem. This causes more harm than good, as you replace action with idle thinking

and don't make any decision -- leading to indecision.

Moreover, in more complex situations, there are few other challenges that one needs to understand:

- Uncertainty of the situation in the future
- Complexity due to multiple factors
- Consequences that have high stakes
- Availability of numerous alternatives
- Interpersonal issues where other persons are affected and thus need to be involved in the decision-making process

Chapter 2: Why do You End up Making Bad Choices?

****

> *"Stubborn and ardent clinging to one's opinion is the best proof of stupidity."*
>
> *– Michel de Montaigne*

Decision making takes a lot out of us. We are nothing but a sum total of our beliefs and consistent thought patterns in our day-to-day lives as we portray any behavior or take different actions.

Therefore, when confronted with choices, it's not only those concretely visible outside factors that make our job taxing, but our deeply rooted beliefs and consistent thought patterns often pose a much bigger challenge. These internal factors are not visible to anyone outside, yet they are hidden mental traps that often get in the way of making smart choices.

In this section, we will get deeper inside our heads and understand the internal hidden traps that lead to ineffective decision making. Researchers John Hammond, Ralph Keeney and Howard Raiffa describe this state in their article, based on years of psychological research on various aspects of decision making.

Let's get started in learning the major hidden traps that affect the quality of our decisions.

Anchoring Trap

Often, we are influenced by the first information presented to us and give disproportionate weight to this option, while considering many options presented later. No matter what comes to us first and is later followed by other choices, unconsciously our decisions are inevitably influenced by the first set of information.

For example, how would you answer the two questions below?

- a. Is the population of Turkey greater than 35 million?
- b. What is your best estimate of the population of Turkey?

There is a huge probability that your answer to the second question will be influenced by the figure mentioned in the first. In fact, the researchers tested the above questions with a large group of people and concluded that, in most cases, the instant answer to the second question was around the first figure. They also tested it by replacing the number by 100 million and, surprisingly, the answers to the second question started to come closer to the new figure.

This simple test illustrates the **basic mental phenomenon known as *anchoring***. When considering any decision, our minds give disproportionate weight to the first information it receives. This information could be in the form of initial impressions, data, or estimates that affect our subsequent thoughts and judgments.

I'm sure that you must have some personal examples of anchoring in your life. Assume you want to travel to another city or country for the first time. As people generally do, you perform a Google search about the people in the territory. If the initial information exposed is "the people in this area are cunning and you need to be careful when dealing with them", then your mind will subconsciously take note of it; and when you travel there, you will carry this first impression about the people in your head. Your interactions and dealings with the people will be influenced by that first impression – and, therefore, all your decisions in dealing with them in that city will be colored by the anchoring trap.

Status Quo Trap

Status quo is a Latin word meaning *"maintaining a situation as it is"*. This trap biases us towards maintaining the current situation, even if better options exist. Humans generally feel comfortable maintaining the status quo, as this offers security. As the saying goes, "a known devil is better than an unknown angel", so people want to continue with their current status, as making any change will expose them to uncertainty.

An example. Some people are highly risk averse and always put their surplus funds in low but fixed interest deposits. Now such people will continue to make the same decision time and again despite being presented with more rewarding investment options. When posed with a new option, they might say they will think about it later, but that "later" never comes, and they continue to accept the measly returns on their investment year after year because they get too much comfortable with the status quo.

An experiment was conducted in which two groups of people were offered two different gifts of equivalent value – half of them received a mug, while the other half received a Swiss chocolate bar. They were then asked to exchange their gifts with the other group. The researchers expected around 50% of the people to happily make the exchange. But, surprisingly, the results showed that only 10% percent exchanged their gifts – that strong is the desire of people to maintain their existing situations.

People maintain the status quo because they feel comfortable and safe with the known. For them, trying something new means uncertainty, discomfort, and risk; therefore, maintaining the status quo is their natural reaction. The status quo trap affects our decision to try a newer and better option.

Sunk Cost Trap

One of our natural tendencies is to perpetuate the mistakes of the past. We tend to justify our past choices even though we see evidence that they are no longer valid. People buy real estate or some other investment and come to the realization that it is a bad one, but still they continue to hold that investment in the hope that the market will correct and eventually make up for the losses. But, unfortunately, even if the market continues to tumble, they still stay invested in their original decisions.

Take another example. People choose a specific career and a few years later, they realize that they do not want to pursue it any further. But by that time, they have already invested so much time, effort, and energy that it becomes very hard to shift careers.

I have personally gone through these phases. After spending more than one and a half decade in the corporate world, it was a temptation to continue with that career. But, somehow, the drive to explore newer ways of living was stronger than continuing on my existing path, so I took the plunge to the world of entrepreneurship.

But the majority of the population keeps justifying their past decisions and don't make new ones. Why do they behave so? Because taking a new approach means admitting that our past decisions were wrong, and, frankly speaking, people are reluctant to admit to a mistake.

That's the reason a manager finds it difficult to fire an underperforming employee, because firing would indicate that the manager had made a wrong hiring decision. So, the manager continues with the underperforming employee, even though that decision compounds the original error.

In the corporate world, if an organization shows a trend of imposing severe penalties for past mistakes, then employees wouldn't change their courses of action and perpetuate past decisions in the hope that the current situation will improve. Admitting mistakes can have dire consequences, so people choose to continue adhering to their past wrongs.

Confirming Evidence Trap

This trap leads one to seek out information that supports existing beliefs while discounting any opposing information.

A psychological study was conducted with two groups of people: one group was in favor of the death penalty for deterring crime, while the other was against it. Both groups were provided with two detailed research papers on the effectiveness of the death penalty in deterring crime. One report established that the death penalty is effective, while the other concluded that it is not.

The results of the experiment showed that despite being aware of detailed scientific research with arguments and counter-arguments regarding the death penalty, each group became more convinced about the validity of their own position. People simply accept information that supports their pre-conceived notions and dismiss conflicting information.

Why does this happen?

It is our tendency to subconsciously decide what we want to do before we even figure out why we want to do it. We are naturally inclined to engage ourselves in the things we like rather than in the things we don't like. Thus, we find arguments for what we like and simply reject information that doesn't support our likings. Chip Heath, author of the book, *Decisive,* rightly states: ***"When people have the opportunity to collect information from the world, they are more likely to select information that supports their pre-existing attitudes, beliefs, and actions."***

Framing Trap

This trap plagues us when we make the mistake of framing a problem or question appropriately. The way a problem is defined can significantly influence one's choices.

The same problem can elicit very different responses when framed using a different reference point. Let's assume that you have $2,000 in your bank account and are asked the following questions:

- Would you accept a fifty-fifty chance of either losing $300 or winning $500?
- Would you accept the chance?

What if you were asked this question?

- Would you prefer to keep your checking account balance of $2,000 or accept a fifty-fifty chance of having either $1,700 or $2,500 in your account?

You can see that the two questions pose the same problem. While your answers to both should, rationally speaking, be the same, studies have shown that many people refuse the 50:50 chance in the first question but accept it in the second. These different reactions result from the different reference points presented.

Therefore, the way any question is framed has an immediate impact on the way you will make a decision.

Recallability Trap

This trap gives undue weight to recent and dramatic events. As humans, we tend to give more importance to recent memories and events with the most effect. We frequently base our predictions of future events based on past memories and events that are either recent or have some dramatic element attached to them.

A study by Karlsson, Loewenstein, and Ariely (2008) showed that people are more likely to purchase insurance to protect themselves after a natural disaster they have just experienced than they are to purchase insurance on this type of disaster before it happens. Their decisions are influenced by the recency of events and recallability of the information.

Let's take an example, say you have to decide and finalize your next vacation location, and you have several options in mind. But suddenly, you remember that you recently heard about a heinous rape and murder incident that appeared on the news channels. Now, even if that country has high security measures and zero-tolerance policies regarding tourist safety and protection, your first inclination is to base your decisions on the most recent dramatic event instilled in your memory, prompting you to skip going on vacation to this country in favor of another one.

All of these hidden traps unknowingly come in the way of decision making. If one is not aware of internal self-sabotaging biases over a long period of time, they can lead to bad decisions. But once you are aware of them, you become more objective in your assessments and take different perspective before arriving at any decision.

Chapter 2- Key Takeaways

It's not only the outside factors that make decision making difficult, but there are many internal hidden traps that trip us and lead to bad choices:

- **Anchoring Trap: Our minds are influenced by the first set of alternatives, and this colors all other future alternatives**. Any marketer would offer you an initial price of 97$, before discounting it and finally selling it to you for 27$, because the anchoring trap makes you believe that you are getting 97$ worth value for just 27$. So beware of this trap.

- **Status Quo Trap**: Human beings love certainty and the security of the future. For most people, trying something new means uncertainty, discomfort, and risk; therefore, **maintaining the status quo is their natural reaction.**

- **Sunk Cost Trap**: After making a wrong decision, people often continue with it for a much longer time, instead of correcting it. Changing the course of action causes a big dent in one's ego, as it implies that we made the wrong decision earlier, and that's not easy to accept for most. Moreover, if it has huge consequences, people avoid admitting to their mistakes and continue with the hope that the situation will improve.

- **Confirmation Evidence Trap**: When we have an existing belief about something, we don't want to listen to an alternate view; rather, we try to find evidence that support our pre-existing belief. Due to this trap, we don't try newer things and explore better opportunities, because we are **more focused on proving ourselves right, rather than choosing something that's actually right.**

- **Framing Trap:** Our ability to respond to any situation is strongly influenced by the way the situation is framed. If the framing shows a bigger advantage or pleasure or avoids some big pain or problem, we are immediately inclined to make a decision, as compared to situations that are framed in a way that is not very clear or precise, or does not evoke emotions.

- **Recallability Trap**: We are influenced more by the recency of events and those situations that we can recall immediately. This leads to **assigning undue weight to current situations and all but ignoring events or situations we don't recollect** – meaning we don't take into account the insights gained from our distant past and, thus, make faulty decisions.

Chapter 3: Understand and Improve Your Decision-Maker Archetype

****

> *"Decision is the spark that ignites action. Until a decision is made, nothing happens. Decisions are the courageous facing of issues, knowing that if they are not faced, problems will remain forever unanswered."*
>
> *~Wilferd Peterson*

We see all the time that a few people make decisions pretty fast while most of the population seem to take ages when even choosing a casual outfit or a regular meal at a restaurant.

Do you wonder why this happen? Is there some difference in the decision making approach by these two sets of people? What is the key driver that fast tracks the decision making process even in the face of complex choices?

Barry Schwartz, an American psychologist, states that **one of the most important elements that governs the decision making approach of different people is the end objective,** and that significantly affects the quality and pace of decision making.

Behind every decision of a decision maker, there is some purpose or objective. Depending upon the end objective desired from any particular decision, there can be four categories of decision makers. Let's understand each of them; and by the end of this chapter, you'll be in a position to identify what category you fall into.

Here are the four categories of decision makers on the criterion of the end objective.

Maximizer

A Maximizer is someone whose end objective is always to look out and opt for the best alternative. Therefore, such a person spends enough time to find as many alternatives as possible before making a decision. After thoroughly analyzing different alternatives on the basis of different parameters, he or she makes a decision and takes the next steps.

But here is the challenge of following this approach. Although they are fully aware that they made the best choice after a thorough analysis, if these people come across something better (than what they decided), they start to question their previous choices and start looking at the new alternatives. Although they made their first decisions thoroughly after taking into consideration the available alternatives, the moment something better is presented to them, they feel discontented with the previous choices and shift their attention to the next best thing.

To put it simply, Maximizers don't remain satisfied even after making the best choice; rather, they want to maximize their benefits all the time.

Let's understand this with the help of an example. Assume you have already purchased a pretty decent outfit from one of the best apparel stores in town to attend a party. But the next day, if you see a different outfit in another store better than what you had bought, you start doubting your previous decision. Since you found the next best alternative, you start feeling bad about your decision despite the fact that that the previous alternative met your requirements.

The Maximizer tasks himself with making the most informed and intelligent decisions after exploring the best possible alternatives. If you seek and accept only the best, you are a Maximizer. Maximizers need assurance that every purchase or decision they make is the best possible.

Moreover, Maximizers want to maximize the benefits of their choices on a consistent basis all the time. You'll be able to better understand this archetype after you compare it with other archetypes of decision makers. So, let's move on to the next one now.

Satisficer

The next type of decision maker is called the Satisficer. The concept of "satisficing" was proposed by U.S. Nobel Prize winning economist, Herbert A. Simon, **by combining the two words "satisfying" and "sufficing".**

Satisficers are **people with a specific criteria or parameters to be fulfilled for making decisions.** Of course, they choose parameters that require exploring the best available alternatives; but unlike Maximizers, they set a specific standard and whatever alternative meets their preset criteria to make a final decision.

Here is the key difference between Satisficers and Maximizers: once Satisficers make a decision based on their own set of standards, they are happy with the decision; and if some other alternative pops up, they don't get disturbed or become dissatisfied with their previous decision, unless and until their earlier decision fails to meet their standard or criteria.

Let's understand this with the help of an example. Assume you want to buy a new car. You have thought of certain key features you want in your car – like engine specifications, specific safety requirements or leg-room, etc. With this preset criterion in your mind, now you start researching and compiling various available alternatives.

Once you find a vehicle that addresses your standards of type of engine, safety or space, you make a decision to buy a particular vehicle and don't bother about other options that might come up later, despite the fact that later options may have some additional features available. You are content with your decision, because it meets your preset standards or parameters for making that particular choice.

To put it simply, **a Satisficer settles for something that is good enough and doesn't worry about the possibility that something better may come up later.** Therefore, a Satisficer keeps on searching for various alternatives based on his or her preset standards; and the moment it is found, he or she stops searching further and makes a decision.

To determine their optimal decision outcome, Maximizers feel compelled to examine each and every alternative available. Maximizers rely heavily on external sources for evaluation. Rather than asking themselves if they enjoy their choice, they are more likely to evaluate their choices based on reputation, social status, and other external cues. By contrast, **Satisficers ask whether their choices are excellent and meet their needs, not whether they are really "the best."**

But don't assume here that Satisficers settle for low standards; their criteria can be very high; but as soon as they find the right alternatives, be it a house, car, or food with the qualities they want, they make their decisions and remain satisfied and don't fret over other later alternatives that pop up.

Perfectionist

Perfectionists are those who keep on exploring their options until they find the "perfect" alternative. They strive for flawlessness and set high performance standards, accompanied by critical self-evaluations and concerns regarding others' evaluations of their performance.

Perfectionists take on stress compulsively toward unattainable goals and measure their self-worth by productivity and accomplishment.

The Perfectionist likes to achieve the best, similar to the Maximizer. But there is a key difference. While both have a high standard of performance, **Perfectionists have very high standards that *they don't expect to meet*. By contrast, Maximizers have very high standards and *they expect to meet*.**

Optimalist

Now comes the last category of decision makers — the Optimalist. **An Optimalist is someone who is mindful of and deals with the constraints of reality**. They know that nothing will ever be perfect, so they are a kind of *ambitious Satisficer.*

In a sense, the Optimalist is not satisfied with good enough; they are ambitious and want more. But at the same time, they are **not *maniac Maximizers***. They are somewhere in between Maximizers and Satisficers.

Which One is Ideal to Strive For?

To start with, Maximizers will never be happy, because the moment they see something better than what they have already chosen, they start regretting their past decisions. No matter how great a decision made, if Maximizers discover something better, they will always regret having failed to choose it in the first place. **Maximizers are prone to experience a**

sense of *"buyer's remorse"* following any purchase decision.

To avoid the kind of regret the Maximizer faces, perfection is comparatively a better approach, because Perfectionists know they have standards they are not expected to meet. But, unfortunately, perfection is not achievable – the journey to perfection is endless, exhaustive, and paralyzing in the constant consideration of multiple alternatives. So the Perfectionist is not happy with their decisions, but they are still better than Maximizers.

John Wooden, an American basketball coach, once said that perfection is what you're striving for, but *perfection is impossibility*. However, *striving for perfection is not impossibility*. Therefore, he advised to do the best you can under the conditions that exist: that is what counts.

You can't achieve perfection; you can only strive for perfection and thus keep on improving. But compared to Maximizers and Perfectionists, Satisficers' stakes are not that high. Therefore, the possibility of regret in the case of the Satisficer is much less, in fact, almost negligible; for them perfection is unnecessary.

The last category of Optimalist is something everyone should strive for, because an Optimalist is really considerate of the hard core realities of what is achievable and what is not, what is controllable and what is not. They know that things can't be perfect, so they choose to perfection; but they won't face regret like Maximizers.

Chapter 3- Key Takeaways

The quality and speed of your decisions will depend on the end objective behind any decision. Based on the end objective approach, we can categorize decision makers into four different types of archetypes:

1. **Maximizer**: They are thorough researchers and explore the best possible alternatives to arrive at a decision; but, sadly, despite arriving at the best decision, they start fretting about, if they come across some other better alternative. **They want to maximize their results all the time, so every new shiny object can easily make them unhappy and dissatisfied** – NOT a good archetype to be.

2. **Satisficer**: Satisficers first decide their parameters and standards for making decision- and these

standards can be high. They look for alternative based on their parameter requirements, and once an alternative meets their requirement, they make a decision. **The best part is, once they make a decision, they are satisfied and don't get disturbed by another better alternatives**, unless the prior choice fails to meet their standards or they evolve and eventually improve their standard. **This is a better approach to decision making that allows you to stay happy and contented with your decision.**

3. **Perfectionist**: They set standards that are too high and even they themselves don't expect to meet. Always straining for making flawless choices and affected by others' opinions on these choices, they take on stress compulsively toward unattainable goals and measure their self-worth by productivity and accomplishment. **They end up not making any decisions because they can't achieve perfection; they can only strive for it. Avoid this trap, because "done is way better than perfect."**

4. **Optimalist**: This is the best archetype one should strive for. Optimalists are considerate of the hard core realities of what is achievable and what is not. They know what is controllable and what is not. They know that things can't be perfect, so they choose to strive for perfection; but they won't face regret like Maximizers or Perfectionists. **They are not maniac Maximizers (always running behind next shiny objects). Rather, they are ambitious Satisficers (setting ever higher stretchable standards and striving to attain them).**

Chapter 4: Effective Techniques to Eradicate Erroneous Thinking

****

"The confidence people have in their beliefs is not a measure of the quality of evidence but of the coherence of the story the mind has managed to construct."

~ Daniel Kahneman

Though we might think so, but making a decision is not merely a rational and logical process of simply choosing between one out of a few options. Most often, you make decisions that have nothing to do with logic; rather, they are carried out based on your own prejudices or biases about the situation, circumstances, or people around you.

One such prevalent bias is confirmation bias, considered as the mother of all biases, and most people suffer from this prejudice. Under this bias, whenever you are presented with some new idea or thought, you simply try to find evidence that confirms your previous beliefs and negates all other information. The point is that the confirmation bias plagues your thinking in a way that becomes a myopic view; you look only for evidence that supports your pre-existing beliefs.

One of the world's best-known sceptics and critical thinkers, Michael Shermer, author of The Believing Brain, has explored the reasoning of people who are stuck in their beliefs. He puts it bluntly: "We form our beliefs for a variety of subjective, personal, emotional, and psychological reasons in the context of environments created by family, friends, colleagues, culture, and society at large; after forming our beliefs we then defend, justify, and rationalize them with a host of intellectual reasons, cogent arguments, and rational explanations. Beliefs come first, explanations for beliefs follow."

I have covered many such biases that stick in your mind and how you can debug them in my other book, *Mind Hacking Secrets*, where you'll learn about a lot of cognitive biases in much greater detail. Now in this section, we will talk about a few mental biases or false assumptions that inhibit the objective decision-making process. I will briefly explain various mental biases and then talk about ways to conquer them.

Unconscious Associations Trigger Wrong Decisions

How unconscious associations influence your actions?

Unconscious associations **influence your actions** in a very specific way. If you unconsciously associate yourself with someone, your decisions and actions will change accordingly. These unconscious associations tend to form over a period of time when staying in a similar environment for a long time. Your environment makes you think about yourself in a particular way – forming a self-imposed identity. There is a famous saying: "*Identity precedes activity.*"

There was a 1998 study[a] conducted on a group of people. The subjects were asked to play Trivial Pursuit (a board game popular in Canada and the US) to test their general knowledge. But the experiment involved one specific element. Before starting the game, the participants were divided into two groups and asked to perform an imagination exercise. The first group was asked to imagine themselves as professors and think like professors. The second group was asked to imagine themselves and think like soccer hooligans.

The result showed that the performance of the two groups differed. The group that thought like an "intelligent" professor got more right answers than the group that thought like "dumb" football hooligans. Regardless of their level of general knowledge before the game, their association with a specific identity significantly influenced their performance.

Malcolm Gladwell in his book, Blink, notes: "[Experiments] suggest that what we think of as free will is largely an illusion: much of the time, we are simply operating on automatic pilot, and the way we think and act – and how well we think and act on the spur of the moment – are a lot more susceptible to outside influences than we realize."

The key takeaway here is to disengage from negative mental associations and, rather, form more powerful positive associations. If you don't have some skill, don't form a negative association of yourself with a poor performer. Rather, opt for online classes or start speaking to mentors and generate a positive association of yourself as a person with a growth mindset who is a keen learner. This simple approach of looking at yourself differently will definitely help you change your actions.

How unconscious associations influence your behavior?

Unconscious associations not only can change our course of action, but they also have the power to **influence our behavior**. There is a general tendency among a large portion of population to unconsciously and automatically associate attributes like "white," "male" and "tall" with qualities like power and competence. Although we may not explicitly admit that tall, white men are more competent than short, black women, but due to this unconscious association, our behavior when dealing with these two sets of people varies.

In fact, one study showed that it is easier to be professionally successful as a tall, white male. A 2004 study by psychologist, Timothy A. Judge, Ph.D., of the University of Florida, and researcher, Daniel M. Cable, Ph.D., of the University of North Carolina, found that **a one-inch increase in height turns into a measurably higher salary, and top management positions are almost exclusively held by white males of above-average height**.

Another classic example of such an unconscious association is Warren Harding, a former US president. He is evidence of how associating general external characteristics with certain skills can turn out to be a blunder. Harding was elected President of the United States after the end of World War I because his supporters simply thought he looked like a president -- because he was a tall, white man. But, apparently, he had no real skills or merits; and as often reported[3], he is widely considered one of the worst presidents of all time. People elected him based on the unconscious association or assumption that white, tall men possess traits that make for a high- profile position.

Unfortunately, unless we are self-aware of these limitations, they strongly influence our actions and behavior unknowingly. Therefore, you need to objectively test your specific assumptions on pre-determined parameters, rather than being misguided by unconscious associations.

The best solution is to become aware of such associations, and this awareness comes by asking questions about different unconscious assumptions. Improving our awareness about these associations will improve the decision-making process.

Avoid the Liking or Mirroring bias -- Stop Being Manipulated

Have you ever had the experience where a buying decision was influenced merely by the salesperson saying something good about you? Salespersons often use such tactics. Try to remember an instance when you were out buying an outfit for a wedding in your family and a sales clerk told you, "This dress suits you well", or maybe "you've made a very good choice". Maybe you didn't realize it at that time, but there are good chances that similar behavior influenced your decision to buy from that salesperson, flattery often has a great impact on our behavior.

This kind of influence on behavior is called the **"liking bias"**. We generally fall prey to this bias – i.e., liking people similar to us and who like us. *__Psychology in the field of sales shows that people tend to buy only from people they like.__*

If you have the choice of buying groceries or cosmetics from two shops, you'll unconsciously choose to go to a store you like or where you feel comfortable with the representatives. If you think that the store manager of a particular store is polite, respectful, and cheerful, you'll be more inclined to buy from that store. That's why in sales training, salespersons are explained the importance of behaving well and maintaining a level of connection with customers, so they can sell more.

Another technique sales people use is *"mirroring,"* or copying the gestures, facial expressions and language of the client. For example, if your manner of expression is through hands movements or using a specific kind of language, and the person in front of you uses the same gesture or language, you immediately start to feel a connection or instant rapport with that person.

I personally experienced this quite a number of times during my stint in a corporate job in Mumbai, the western part of India. I didn't know the local language (Marathi). One of the key thing I noticed was that most of the time while interacting with government officials, like the police or other officials, if someone talked to them in the local language, they seemed to build an instant connection. The outcome was that the officers appeared much more forthcoming to help and offer solutions to their problems. My office colleagues would often talk to them about official work only in the local language, which helped to instantly build rapport. It was clear evidence of "mirroring" in action.

Mirroring helps salespeople appear similar to their clients, thus more likeable and more likely to close the deal. Hence, don't let others affect your decisions to your disadvantage through the ploy of mirroring. You might be realizing by now that merely by knowing about these psychological biases of "liking" and "mirroring", your decisions will start improving.

However, you might try these biases to influence others when selling your ideas or thoughts (with genuine intent and without manipulating), if you want to get along with people instantly and make faster progress.

Use the Observers Perspective for Objective Decisions

Often, the way we make decisions for others is not the same as we would make for ourselves. We give advice to others that we personally wouldn't implement so easily. For example, if a friend, who just took a new job, seeks advice about approaching her manager and explains her inability to fully understand an office-related project, most probably, you would do the following. You would check whether she had tried other ways to resolve the issues on her own. Assuming she answered in the affirmative, your quick advice would be to directly approach the manager and seek clarification.

That seems like a pretty obvious advice, doesn't it? However, assume you had a similar work-related problem. Would you still do the same thing? Probably, you would not be that quick to approach your manager, unless you had a very friendly relationship with him or her. You might hesitate due to the fear of being rejected. You might fear being considered naïve or become anxious thinking that your boss might mistake your lack of knowledge for incompetency.

The reality is: when you personally experience some problem and want to make a decision about it, your decisions are influenced by your emotions. But you don't come across such emotions when you advise others in making similar decisions. This is because while advising your best friend, you would tend to objectively examine the situation and offer an independent opinion. You don't feel the emotions your friend experienced in a particular situation and, therefore, your advice now is to a large extent objective and rational.

Here is the **best piece of guidance we can give when you are indecisive about a situation – follow the observer's approach**. Try to think about how you would look at the situation as an independent person. Try to imagine what you would advise your best friend in such a scenario.

The observer approach will help you form an unbiased and unprejudiced view of the situation, and you can make decisions faster this way. This approach gives you solutions from an objective perspective, as if advice received from an outside independent point of view.

Shift Autopilot behavior to Manual Behavior

Most often, due to behaving in a particular way for a long period, we start to behave that way almost on an autopilot basis. When we do certain actions day after day on a mechanical basis, we don't notice the gradual changes that, over time, can lead to a drastic situation.

To avoid this mental trap, **we need a figurative "tripwire"**, a signal that makes us aware of our autopilot behavior and, if necessary, prompts us to correct it. One way to this is to establish clear signals to interrupt any "autopilot behavior", because by repeating that behavior an infinite number of times, you become so numb that minor nudges don't work anymore. So, you need some kind of tripwire arrangement that will provoke a kind of shock that immediately disturbs your autopilot thinking pattern.

Let's take an example of a tripwire that the American shoe seller, Zappos, follows systematically. Zappos has a program that pays new employees $4,000 to quit the company during the initial training session. The policy is designed to make sure new employees are committed to working at the online retailer beyond just a paycheck. This move ensures that once new employees feel they don't like working there anymore, they're encouraged to take the money and leave.

This is a tripwire to help staff see their situation clearly. It interrupts the indecisive behavior of otherwise unmotivated employees based on habit and prompts conscious decision-making. This is a win-win proposition because on the one hand, it helps unmotivated staff make a decision and on the other hand, it helps Zappos get rid of underperforming personnel.

Change Behavior with Deadlines or Partitions

Another trick to change your autopilot behavior is to create deadlines to keep yourself from falling into bad habits. Deadlines help enforce a decision we'd otherwise procrastinate on.

One of the six elements of influence, as propounded by Robert Cialdini in his great book, *Influence,* is the element of scarcity or urgency. As humans, we even don't take the best action for us when there is no urgency -- that's how humans behave. We keep on delaying even if we know that a decision is best for us, thinking we will do it later. But as soon as we realize that we will miss out on the chance to avail ourselves of some offer, we immediately take action. Deadlines trigger the autopilot behavior of not taking action.

Along these lines, another study was conducted where the researchers offered college students $5 to fill out a survey. Initially, they were not given a timeframe. Despite the fact that they would receive money to fill out the survey, the students were not forthcoming. Later, when given a five-day deadline to complete the survey, 66% of the students collected the money; but without a deadline, only 25% collected it.

Another effective approach to trigger behavior is *to make partitions*, meaning dividing the reward in various parts to keep incentivizing the action.

For instance, if you look at the venture capital investment world, instead of handing out one huge sum to entrepreneurs, large investments are distributed by dispensing smaller sums over time.

This is done to prompt the conscious attention of the entrepreneur, serving as a tripwire that doesn't let people get into their comfort zone and slack off. Therefore, each round of partial investment serves as a tripwire to make sure that everything is going the right way.

Let's talk about one last method that works to get people out of their autopilot behavior. It is by way of **using labels to recognize disturbing (or encouraging) patterns**. For example, in their training, pilots are introduced to the concept of *leemers*, which describes *"the vague feeling that something isn't right, even if it's not clear why."* Having a name for this feeling means that pilots are less likely to ignore their feelings. **Once a name is given to the feeling, its existence is acknowledged**. It becomes important because when they are responsible for the lives of so many people, even a nagging feeling can act as a tripwire prompting them to pay conscious attention to the situation.

To sum up, being aware of your internal biases and using strategies to overcome them will help you make better and more effective decisions. Even knowing these biases exist will give an edge over other people who are unaware of them.

Now let's move on to the next chapter, where we will learn how much information we should look for in order to make effective decisions.

Chapter 4- Key Takeaways

Humans wrongly believe themselves to be rational beings, while truth is most of our decisions are influenced by pre-existing beliefs formed based on our life circumstances, past experiences and emotional state when making decisions.

Many techniques help us avoid making faulty decisions:

- **Be aware of unconscious association**: Our unconscious associations about our own identity or that of other persons formed on the basis of surrounding environment or past experiences influences our behavior and actions when making different decisions. **The best solution to overcome this to become aware of such associations.** This awareness comes from asking questions about different unconscious assumptions. Merely awareness of these associations can significantly improve our decision-making.

- **Handle the liking and mirroring Bias**: Marketers tend to influence our buying decisions by flattering or mirroring our gestures, as everyone loves to be praised and liked. **To avoid being manipulated and take the right decisions, you should be more watchful of such behavior** and if needed, seek guidance from someone who is independent and has not any vested interest in the offer.

- **Use the observer perspective**: You may often be quick to give advice to others in different situations, if you are not emotionally involved in their situations. However, when you have to make your own decisions in similar situations, it's difficult to follow that advice. **The best solution here is to disengage yourself from your situation and look at it from an observer's perspective** to get an objective and independent view of the situation.

- **How to shift from autopilot to manual behavior**: Humans are creatures of habit and routine; followed for a long time, it becomes autopilot like brushing your teeth. **To avoid making decisions on an autopilot basis, you need to give a tripwire or shock to your mind** – anything that forces you think differently and trigger different behavior.

- **Change behavior with deadlines/partitions**. Offering deadlines to a particular activity or assigning a series of milestones to any major goal is a perfect strategy to stay alert and come out of autopilot behavior.

Chapter 5: Why You Don't Always Need More Information?

****

"The key to good decision making is not knowledge. It is understanding. We are swimming in the former. We are desperately lacking in the latter."

— Malcolm Gladwell

A good decision requires an optimal amount of information. Too much information and you'll be trapped in paralysis by analysis and eventually end up failing to make any choice. On the other hand, too little information, and you'll be stressed and anxious about your decision going wrong.

Therefore, the important questions one needs to ponder about are:

- How much information do you really need before making a decision?
- What kind of information must you consider as necessary and what information can be easily ignored as irrelevant?

In this chapter, we will discuss some of the best techniques to optimize your approach to gathering the most relevant information.

Don't Always Decide in Yes or No

Although doing so saves time and makes you sound more efficient in decision-making, you don't have to always make decisions in the form of yes or no. In fact, it is not advisable in some cases to make decisions in this way. Moreover, sometimes you want to say "no", but the person asking is in a dominant position and saying "no" could be dangerous. Let's try to understand this concept with the help of few examples.

Suppose your best friend asks you to accompany her to a movie over the weekend, and obviously you find it difficult to answer directly in yes or no. Saying yes to this option might require you to reschedule other pre-commitments, while on the other hand, refusing your friend will make you feel like you are sacrificing your desire for entertainment; and probably your best friend won't be very happy (she will be rather annoyed) if you simply reject her by saying a direct "NO".

Then what should you do?

Here is another perspective on the situation in a pragmatic manner, so it becomes a win-win game for both of you. Without getting into the pressure of quickly saying yes or no, rather, think whether there are other alternatives besides watching a movie during that time your friend has proposed going out for movie.

Maybe you are celebrating an evening out with family over dinner or have a get together with a few old friends to share their life experiences. You might ask her to join you. You can even suggest a visit to a book fair or an exhibition that you think is a better and more enriching experience than watching some movie just for entertainment. Remember, you always have many choices instead of limiting yourself to the simple option of yes or no.

Take another situation. Assume your manager hands over a new work assignment when your desk is already crying (on the verge of breaking with the load of files). Can you say "no" directly? If your manager happens to be a friend, maybe you can take a chance and say "no", but that's more of the exception than the rule. You want to say "no", but you might have to do so unwillingly.

In the above situation, you can also think of proposing an alternative. You could tell your manager that "X" and "Y" projects need to be delivered to key management by the next day, and then ask her whether project "Z" is more urgent. You might seek some additional time for project X and Y, if project Z is more important. Or you can ask for support from other team members to help you finish the new project within the deadline.

It's when you think about other alternatives then only you can avoid getting into the trap of saying simply "yes" or "No". People are generally unconscious of other options or alternatives but know that you can handle the matter in an effective way by proposing them. It works in most cases.

A study conducted at Southwestern University in Texas involved 150 students in an experiment. The results demonstrated that when student participants were given a choice between buying a video they liked for $14.99 or not buying it at all, only 25% didn't buy it. Since most of them liked the videos, they unconsciously went ahead and bought them.

Then researchers made a small change in the negative option. Instead of simply saying no, the wordings of the negative choice also stated, *"keep the $14.99 for another purchase."* The results were significantly different with this slight change. 45% of the students didn't buy the video this time.

Since the choice itself remained the same in both cases, this example shows that just a subtle suggestion about the existence of another alternative is enough to improve decision-making. In terms of economics, this concept is known as **"opportunity cost" – meaning other opportunities you would lose by exercising the present option.**

Therefore, if the decision to be made is posed in terms of "take it or leave it", you'll be forced to choose it or reject it. But if you are slightly nudged toward other alternatives, it will expand your thinking horizon, and now you will consider these alternatives as well.

Remember, your best decisions always come from one of the many options. Therefore, don't restrict yourself to just a yes or no decision; but expand your alternatives, and chances are you will come across some other alternative that's the best utilization of your time and effort.

Multi-tracking of Information

Most people try to solve a problem by implementing the one option that seems best. However, studies show that trying out just a few more options simultaneously can yield much better results. The approach of trying multiple options together is known as **multi-tracking**, and it has the potential to improve one's cognitive abilities and thus the decision-making process significantly.

In one research experiment, two groups of graphic designers were given the assignment of making a banner advertisement for an online magazine. The first group created just one advertisement at a time, receiving feedback after each round. The second group, however, began their process with three ads, to which they received direct feedback from the client; and then they narrowed the choice down to two options. On the basis of the next feedback round, they arrived at a definitive result.

The ads of the second group were rated higher by magazine editors, independent ad executives, and in real-world tests. Why was this so? By simultaneously working on several ideas, the designers in the second group were in an advantageous situation, as they were able to directly compare the feedback on each design during each round of work, and, thus, they could incorporate the client's suggestions on three different designs constructively into one single ad.

Multi-tracking not only can result in higher-quality work, but as studies have shown, exploring several alternatives at the same time actually speeds up the decision-making process.

Another reason this works is because by having more alternatives, you're less invested in any single option, which allows you to remain flexible with either option, whereas if you work only on one design, you'll be highly invested in the success of that design, adversely affecting your flexibility.

I closely relate the above study with my personal experience while engaging designers for my book covers. I have one designer, who always responds with two different sets for each book cover. It helps me see two different alternatives at one go. With this flexibility, I can either select one out of the two options or I can pick the best elements of both designs and the let the designer know my feedback for further changes. Here the designer is more flexible with either of the options to make needed revisions.

To make your decision-making process more effective, try to adopt a few different approaches together. This reminds me of the **principle of Taking Massive Action"**, as suggested by Tony Robbins, the world-renowned strategy coach. How? Working on multiple tracks for one project requires you to put in additional time and effort simultaneously to deliver a variety of options.

Here is the benefit – by working on different options, you put more thinking and effort into the project. You start to see the different ways your project can unfold if you follow multiple approaches simultaneously. Finally, massive action shows your mistakes, if any, in the early stages and, therefore, you can correct your course of action, thereby enriching your experience and making you wiser about better future decisions.

But, don't be too aggressive in this approach. Here is a caution – you need to **avoid the "choice overload" problem**, as you'll learn next.

Avoid Choice Overload

We often say, "the more the merrier," but, unfortunately, it's not true in making choices – when your attention is drawn towards too many choices, this is often a roadmap that leads to the wonderland of indecision. You end up doing nothing when overloaded with too many alternatives.

Companies sometimes assume that if they offer their customers more choices, they'll be more likely to buy their products. They wrongly think their customers will find *exactly* what they like, if there are lot of alternatives to choose from.

But here arises the **paradox of choice**: if a person is presented with too many choices, he or she is actual*ly less likely* to buy. In 2000, psychologists, Sheena Iyengar and Mark Lepper from Columbia and Stanford University, respectively, published research about selling a variety of jams to potential customers. Their research was conducted inside an upmarket grocery store, where they put a jam-tasting booth for store customers to taste different kinds and choose the best.

On one Saturday at rush hour in the grocery store, 24 varieties were presented. However, a week later on Saturday for the same time duration, only six different varieties of jam were presented before consumers. This was done to understand how people respond to a vast catalogue of options versus a limited selected few.

The results of the study were surprising. It showed that in the second experimentation, by showing only six types of jam, the organizers were able **to sell ten times more** compared to the first day. The researchers concluded that while the big display table (with 24 jams) generated more interest, people were far less likely to purchase a jar of jam than in the case of the smaller display of six.

Can you guess the reason behind this? It lies in the way human psychology operates. In the first instance, the customers were overwhelmed with the sheer number of choices presented before them, and they couldn't decide which one they liked the most. In such a situation, the ultimate reaction was not to decide anything -- so they didn't buy. While too many choices seem to be appealing at the first sight, choice overload paralyzed the customers. Instead, when they were presented some limited number of options, they responded pretty well, as making a choice of one or two jars out of six was comparatively much easier and cognitively less taxing.

Therefore, comparing the choice overload concept with the previous technique of multi-tracking, it is definitely better to have a few alternatives simultaneously than just one plan of action. It can be seen, however, that if one is bombarded with too many choices, overwhelm and indecision will be the consequences.

Avoid Irrelevant Information

The immediate attention span of modern man has been drastically reduced thanks to the advent of technology and, most particularly, smartphones loaded with unlimited internet access and an army of mobile applications. A recent study[6] conducted by Microsoft Corporation showed that the human immediate attention span has declined to only *eight* seconds. To give you a comparison, a goldfish (notorious for the worst attention span) has an immediate attention span of *nine* seconds, so humans are now worse off than goldfish in maintaining a short-term attention span.

But here is the thing. To make better decisions, you need to focus your attention on aspects that really matter. You need to avoid or get rid of any information or things that don't contribute positively to your most important decisions. In effect, you need to cut out all irrelevant information.

That's why Apple's Steve Job's closet was filled with dozens of identical black turtlenecks and Levi's 501 jeans -- to simplify his choices. That's why Barack Obama a former U.S. president once said in an interview, "You'll see that I wear only gray or blue suits. I don't want to make decisions about what I'm eating or wearing because I have too many other decisions to make."

Why do all these high-achievers cut short all routine decisions? Because they are well-aware of the concept of **"decision fatigue."** Psychologists explain that our minds have a limited amount of willpower and we consume willpower for making any kind of decision. The more decisions we make, the more willpower is consumed.

A study was conducted in 2011 to examine the factors that influence the decision of judges in Israel in a particular type of case, i.e., granting parole to criminals.

It was noted that during the morning, judges have the tendency to deliver positive rulings that result in approving the parole of criminals almost 65% of the time. But as the morning hours went by, the chances of giving favorable rulings dropped to zero.

Again, immediately after the lunch break, the judges started to give favorable rulings almost

65% of the time. But this percentage moved to zero in the late afternoon. The study established that the judges' quality of decision-making deteriorated by making more decisions, so they started to avoid them.

One important point to note here is that our brain doesn't distinguish between the most important and trivial things in terms of expending energy. It never thinks of safeguarding our willpower by using the less quantity of willpower when, for example, we are choosing our regular meal at a restaurant or selecting the dress we will wear tomorrow morning by labeling these activities as low-value. In other words, it consumes similar amount of willpower for making a trivial choice versus making some important decisions.

Therefore, it is advisable to safeguard your willpower for only those decisions that are most important. One good strategy to avoid irrelevant information called *"Elimination by Aspects Model"* was proposed by Amos Tverskey, a cognitive psychologist. In this approach, you evaluate each of the available alternatives by measuring them with one parameter at a time, beginning with the most important for making the decision. When a particular alternative doesn't meet the parameter you established for your end objective, you instantly delete the item from your list of options. By following this approach sequentially, your list of possible choices gets smaller and smaller, as you eliminate items, until you eventually arrive at just one.

I have come to realize lately that, unknowingly, I have been using this technique for most of my life - for the simplest to the most complex decisions: for example, the technique I used in making the big decision to shift my family to a new city and take up a new challenging job. I gave more weight to my personal growth and didn't give much to the comfort level I could have enjoyed by staying in my own town, where I've resided for decades. While deciding, I eliminated those elements that were less significant and finally closed in on the one that was more important to me.

Also, I have been using the technique in simple matters like helping my spouse shop for outfits (by the way, it's not that simple). Here is what I do. I start by simply eliminating dresses one by one based on how they look on her. She has a fair complexion and, therefore, any dress with lighter shades doesn't suit her compared to bright colors. There is one more aspect: she has a lot of black in her outfit collection; therefore, while choosing based on the process of elimination, any dress with black (howsoever good it looks on her) gets eliminated for this reason. It becomes easier to decide when you eliminate some alternatives based on your pre-set parameters.

In short, this process of elimination by aspects is a great strategy to cut your choices down to an important few, so you don't get paralyzed by choice overload.

Follow the 40:70 Rule

We talked a lot throughout in this chapter about information overload, but in today's complex business world, we also encounter occasions when we are information starved - let's call it **information scarcity.**

Yes, there are times when you have to make decisions in the face of a high degree of uncertainty, because you realize that there is not enough data or information upon which you can base your decisions. A lack of complete information puts you in state of anxiety, and you don't move any further along. How can you be comfortable deciding when you don't have enough data about various aspects of making decisions and how each parameter would interplay with the others?

Information scarcity puts you into a state of inaction, and you get into a phase where you often find yourself telling others you are researching and collecting data to make a decision, but don't decide for long. In such situations, you can use **Colin Powell's 40-70 Rule.** Former U.S. Secretary of State Colin Powell devised this rule as a guidance tool to make decisions when you lack sufficient information.

He suggested that whenever you want to make a decision on an important project that involves uncertainties about future outcomes, **you should have no less than 40% and you don't need more than 70% of the information to make a decision**. He states that less than 40% of information means we are bound to make wrong decisions. If we continue to search for more than 70% information, we end up taking so much time that the decision itself will not deliver meaningful results because it's already too late.

This rule is not some blind hasty suggestion. While it doesn't rely on securing 100% information, it still recommends having a reasonable amount; and a 40-70% ratio is something that can be relied upon, particularly when there are many uncertain factors to take into account.

Chapter 5- Key Takeaways

You really don't need that much quantity of information; rather, you need right quality of information. Here is how to do it.

- **Don't always decide in yes or no**: Deciding always in yes or no is not the best approach, as it sometimes puts you in a stressful situation. Therefore, **instead of agreeing or disagreeing, try to explore other alternatives or possibilities**. When you demand yourself to think beyond yes or no options, you'll generate a few other alternatives to mull over. Once you have other options besides the one presented to you, compare them, and whatever gives the best return for your time and attention, go for it. **Always ask yourself, "Is there any other option?"**

Your time, energy and efforts are limited resources, and there is opportunity cost for not choosing a particular alternative. Therefore, generate more alternatives beyond simple "yes" or "no" and go for the best one.

- **Multi-tracking of information**: Instead of working on one option to solve a problem, the better approach is to work simultaneously on other alternatives. **"Multi-tracking of information"** offers you the benefit of exploring the pros and cons of several options simultaneously. If one option doesn't seem to work, you can immediately switch to another option or produce a combination of the best out of multiple choices. **This sharpens your cognitive abilities, as you will make fine distinctions between different options** by practically working on them simultaneously.

- **Avoid choice overload**: Don't over burden yourself with too many choices. Research shows that the more the number of options, the more difficult it becomes to make decisions. The paradox of choice will overwhelm you, and you'll tend to procrastinate and not take further action.

Please bear in mind that you don't have to always choose between yes or no. It's always recommended to enhance the number of options and follow multi-tracking of information, but you have to be cautious to limit the number of your choices, so you are not plagued by the paradox of choice.

- **Avoid irrelevant information**: Humans have a short attention span, so you need to be wise when exposing yourself to information and eliminate irrelevant stuff. **Avoid decision fatigue** by not wasting your willpower on routine decisions like choosing meals or clothes, and keep it reserved for important issues. **Use the "Elimination by Aspects Model"** and evaluate each piece of available information through the lens of a pre-identified set of parameters based on importance.

If any piece of information doesn't meet important parameters, it needs to be eliminated quickly, and one should focus only on relevant information to speed up the decision making process.

- **Follow the 40:70 rule**: You don't need to wait for 100% of the information to make decisions. **Follow Collin Powell's Rule – if you have information of more than 40% and up to 70% for making any particular decision, don't wait and just make the decision**. There will always be an element of uncertainty in every situation. Waiting until all the uncertainties are crystal clear is a perfectionist tendency, because situations can never be "perfect". Therefore, follow Collin Powell's 40-70% rule and make start making decisions based on your judgement of the limited set of information available.

Chapter 6: A Proactive Smart Choice Approach+ Using Ancient Intelligence (AI)

****

> *"Nobody's life is ever all balanced. It's a conscious decision to choose your priorities every day."*
>
> *~ Elisabeth Hasselbeck*

Some people erroneously think that decision making is some inborn quality or something solely gifted to a selected few. This chapter will help you bust this myth completely, since you will learn the elements of effective decision making. By the end of this chapter, you'll understand that everyone is capable of making better decisions.

There are a few essential elements of decision-making, which if understood well and then implemented in day-to-day choices, will empower you to make better and more effective decisions. Once you are aware of these key elements, you will find that you start to make better decisions. These key elements of effective decision are listed below:

- Effective decision making is focused on _what is important to you._
- It is _logical and consistent_, because it's based on certain pre-set principles.
- It is _holistic_ and takes into account subjective and objective factors related to any problem. It also blends analytical thinking with the intuitive approach.
- It encourages _gathering as much relevant information_ (but not too much) as necessary to form an opinion about a situation.

If you try to analyze any of your good decisions, you will realize that each such decision already contained these prescribed elements. Once you know these key elements of decision making, the next step is to learn an approach or process that will ensure that all the choices you make ultimately contain all the elements of effective decision making.

Let's now discuss the decision-making process that will ensure that we make best decisions for ourselves and others around us.

The PrOACT Approach

A wonderful decision making approach comes from the researchers, John Hammond, Ralph Keeney and Howard Raiffa, in the form of an acronym, PrOACT. Each character of the term PrOACT stands for a specific step in the process for making effective decision:

- **Pr**- Problem Identification
- **O**- Objective Clarification
- **A**- Alternative Expansion
- **C**- Consequences of alternatives
- **T**- Trade-offs to be made between alternatives

You'll realize that this approach is, in fact, a proactive method of decision making after you go through each of the steps below:

Problem Identification

The first step is to determine what exactly the problem is. Let's understand this by way of an example. Assume you want to join a coaching class on an academic or professional subject. How would you identify your problem? You'd probably start simply with the question, "which coaching center should I join?"

But hang on. Is this the real problem or there is another perspective to look at? If you spend a few moments refining it, you'll notice that your key problem is how to learn better and not the selection of a coaching center. With the new approach of defining your problem, you widen your thinking perspective and not limit yourself to merely a location.

You've now identified the problem correctly, i.e., how to learn better and more effectively and, accordingly, you'll start to see the available options. Maybe you want to consider purchasing an online coaching course that you can pursue in the comfort of your home. Or maybe just sitting with some of your like-minded friends and pondering all the problems you encounter related to your studies could be a good idea for finding the solutions in a much collaborative manner.

The objective of this step is to ensure that you don't immediately jump in and start looking for solutions without first really understanding the core of the problem. In order to make a good choice, you have to state your problem very carefully.

Clarify Your Objective

Once you identify your problem correctly, the next step is identifying the end objective you want to achieve by making a decision.

Let's continue with the previous example of joining a coaching class. Once you have started identifying the problem, immediately you begin to ponder the end objective you want to achieve by solving it. You realize that your end objective is to learn effectively, at a reasonable cost and with as little inconvenience as possible. Once you have clarified your objective, you start seeing the same problem from a different perspective.

Take another example. Assume you want to choose between a morning walk or preparing to participate in a half marathon. Here is how you'd operate. If your objective is just to maintain a regular and fit body, you would simply choose to go for a quick walk or jog. But if your objective is to test and stretch your physical limits and run a half or full marathon, then you would decide about adopting the right training regimen with the appropriate diet specifications.

The decision between going for a morning walk as routine exercise versus undergoing professional training for a half marathon depends on the end objective related to your health.

You have to ask yourself what you want to accomplish most and which of your interests, values, concerns, fears, and inspirations are most relevant for achieving that goal. Thinking through your objective will give direction to your decision making.

Expand Your <u>Alternatives</u>

The next step in the PrOACT approach is to create as many alternatives as you possibly can. You need to be imaginative and creative in determining the alternative solutions for any problem. The first step is to write down all of them or cast as wide a net as possible of alternatives that come to mind. I know some of these alternatives might not sound that good when you first list them, but don't fret over these different alternatives. You can strike them off later, when you start analyzing the various options to reach the best one. Sometimes, the alternative that doesn't sound appealing initially turns out to be the best one. So expand your alternatives – because you don't want to lose out on the best alternative.

Take another example. Assume you want your child to choose a particular field of study or career. You need to check the kinds of alternatives you have for him or her based on his skills, interests, strengths, etc.

Ask, how good is your child at school, and how good is he or she in sports or extra-curricular activities? Does he or she love to stay alone or with a few friends, or is he or she has more of an extroverted personality? Considering all these factors will help you create several alternatives. Having a good number of alternatives is important when considering all the possible solutions in front of you.

If you don't have different alternatives, you'll be constantly wondering and worrying whether you have missed out on some possibility. You might also regret later not spending enough time expanding your alternatives before making the final decision.

Therefore, strive for at least a wide range of creative and desirable alternatives because your best decision will only come out of your best alternative.

Understand Consequences

After you have identified multiple alternatives, the next step is to look at the consequences of each one. Assume you are in a corporate job and want to try entrepreneurship. There are different alternatives in front of you. You can do it in the form of a side hustle, doing something early in the morning before you go to office or in the evening after your work hours (I wrote my first two books in the mornings and evenings while working at a full-time day job). Or you may consider jumping full-force into the chosen entrepreneurship by quitting your job.

For each of the alternatives, you have to look at the consequences. If you jump out of the job and start your new venture immediately, it might give you the instant freedom to do what you want. But you need to think about the future of your spouse, kids and other family responsibilities. You should be considerate of what stage of life they're in and what kind of financial security they need, while you are investing time building your empire. You know that leaving a job with a monthly fixed income safety zone for a wild ride of entrepreneurship is not an easy decision. So, you need to weigh the pros and cons to analyze if it is a good option to put your spouse and family in financial jeopardy, or could you do it on the side?

If you are crystal clear about what business you want to start and also have enough savings to run your family and household without compromising their quality of life for the next 2-3 years, of course, after providing for business expenses, then starting a full-time entrepreneurship may not be that risky a proposition. Otherwise, you may think of doing it on the side or until you save enough funds for a rainy day.

You have to look into the consequences of all your options. Accessing the consequences of each will ultimately help you identify those alternatives best suited to meet your end objective.

Consider Trade-offs

The last step in the PrOACT approach is to consider the trade-offs between the various alternatives. You can have different objectives in life and those different objectives might conflict with each other. Look at the previous example. You have the objective of becoming your own boss by starting your own business, but there is the other very important objective of not compromising the quality of life of your family. Sometimes, you have to compromise and take a middle path and sacrifice one or the other.

The trade-off in the above example is to lose sleep by waking up early and working on your side hustle, extracting some time out of family time in the evening to nurture your entrepreneurship dream. But this loss of sleep and the compromise of family time is to ensure eventual financial security and a better life for your family. In most complex decisions, there is no a single, perfect alternative. You have to juggle many balls at the same time. Your job is to choose intelligently among less-than-perfect alternatives. For this purpose, you need to address the trade-offs between different alternatives by taking into account your key priorities.

This approach of the PrOACT model will divide your decision-making process into simpler steps and highlight the most essential parameters to help you decide better. You just need to brainstorm and come out with the answers to each of elements of the PrOACT model.

By following PrOACT approach, you'll feel a sense of satisfaction because you have already considered all the important criteria and foreseeable aspects in order to arrive at your decision. This will improve your confidence, strengthen your decision making muscle and make you wiser about more effective decisions.

Use Ancient Intelligence to Autopilot your decisions

The modern era is an age of AI (artificial intelligence). We talk about the Internet of Things, big data, robots, etc. etc., - let's put it this way, AI is a modern-world buzzword.

Science is already exploring human cloning – creating a genetically identical copy of a human with artificial intelligence that can think and behave like a human. That's the level of technological innovation of toward which we are moving.

AI, however, is not an entirely new concept. The first reference of the term, artificial intelligence, was made in year 1956 at a conference at Dartmouth College in Hanover, New Hampshire. Although one can argue that a lot has changed, **the basic principles of artificial intelligence remain the same**.

Let's understand by way of example how a computerized decision-making process works. Let's say you want to apply two simple principles for maintaining the centralized air-conditioning of your house. You want to turn the cooling off when the temperature goes below 74 degree Fahrenheit and keep the air-conditioning on only if the temperature goes above 78 from midnight to 6 a.m. You feed the decision criteria into your computer based on these two needs – between midnight to 6 a.m. the air-conditioning needs to be switched on only if the temperature goes above 78 degree Fahrenheit or the air-conditioner will be on every time, unless the temperature goes below 74 degrees.

Therefore, by setting certain formulas, you can create a decision making system for a machine that takes into account the necessary data, applies the principle and recommends a decision based on the principle set for it.

This is the simplest example of intelligence created artificially by the human mind through the use of technology. But with technological advancements, many more parameters or criteria of extreme complexities are added to the computer. The concept of the Internet of Things (IOT) is nothing but the expansion of the realm of artificial intelligence, where you connect a network of physical devices, vehicles, home appliances, and other items embedded with electronics, software, sensors, enabling these things to exchange data with each other to make much more complex activities possible through internet connectivity.

Ray Dalio, an American billionaire investor, known to be among the top 100 richest persons alive, runs a private investment banking firm, Bridgewater Associates, one of the world's biggest hedge funds with a portfolio of 160 billion U.S. dollars. If you don't know him, Dalio is a kind of genius, known for integrating a massive amount of historical data about stocks and other financial instruments' trading patterns with computer-driven algorithms **to make investment decisions automatically through machines**. In effect, **Dalio has been able to brilliantly combine *human intelligence* with the *machine intelligence***, thus creating highly powerful algorithms. These algorithms take massive amounts of historical data and trends in trading commodities, stocks or other financial instruments, and based on the information, the algorithms make future profitable trading or investment decisions.

Know this Superior AI -- Ancient Intelligence

But this is not the only form of AI. Let's talk about another type specific to humans. Ray Dalio in his bestseller book, *Principles: Life and Work,* terms this ***Ancient Intelligence*, which is much more powerful than *artificial intelligence***. Let's understand how?

In human brains, there is a portion known as the *basal ganglia*. The role of this organ is to put certain behaviors that we keep doing on a regular basis on autopilot. We can harness the potential of this part of our brain to write algorithms to reprogram this other form of AI.

How can we do it?

The Power of Implementation Intentions

It is with the help of ***implementation intentions***. As in the way you program your air-conditioning system to work by setting the desired algorithm, it's possible for human beings to program themselves through implementation intentions.

Implementation intention is the simple approach of **taking action based on the "if-then" method** It's a self-regulatory strategy in the form of an "if-then" plan that leads to habit formation and behavior modification.

For example, <u>if</u> it's 7 a.m., <u>then</u> it's wake up time. <u>If</u> you have taken bath, <u>then</u> you will sit for silent meditation for 15 minutes. <u>If</u> it is 10 p.m., <u>then</u> it is time to read a great book for 30 minutes before you sleep. Finally, <u>if</u> it's 10.30 p.m., <u>then</u> you need to go to bed.

Above are simple illustrations of implementation intention that indicate **that *if one condition happens or is satisfied, then you have to take some specific action.*** You set the algorithm for your human machine like this only and then they follow.

The *if-then* approach triggers your basal ganglia to track your behavior for a certain period; and soon it puts you on autopilot. This means that things start to happen on an autopilot basis after you have given it some amount of time to settle in.

This approach of setting algorithms based on your ancient intelligence starts with smaller activities, of course. But as you start adding many "if-then" algorithms through the use of this ancient intelligence, your decision making abilities will enhance. Smaller decisions don't take much time for you, as you have generated a huge subconscious repertoire of many implementation intentions.

Once you set the simpler implementation intentions, you can start accumulating the algorithms for higher decisions like what is the right way to influence your customers' decisions, what products you need to launch in a new market or what would be the right criteria for diversifying your business operations.

And that's the ultimate AI.

Dalio states that traditional AI programming can increase productivity to 100,000 times. Here is how it works. If you make a decision to do the optimal thing once, you save the effort and an enormous amount of willpower of deciding 1,000+ times. You make *100* wise decisions like that, and you have just increased your optimizing efficiency 100,000 fold.

Your ancient intelligence can be programmed the way you want, through consistent repetition with the help of implementation intentions. Once you have been reprogrammed based on your "ancient intelligence", you save enough energy to make bigger and more complex decisions, as you start making smaller and routine decisions based on your internal pre-set programming.

On the top of this, if someone can explore ways of combining ancient intelligence with artificial machine intelligence, the way Dalio does in his own trading decisions, then you can make a huge number of decisions in quite a lesser amount of time. That's the way to explode your growth potential, because, ultimately, life is all about making decisions: the more you make, the better you become.

Chapter 6- Key Takeaways

Before you make any decision, you must understand the key elements of each decision. Effective decision making is:

- focused on *what's important* to you
- *should be logical and consistent*
- should be *holistic* and takes into all elements
- *encourages gathering as much relevant information as necessary*

Follow the PrOACT Approach: PrOACT is an acronym, where each character explains the process of effective decision making as below:

- **Problem Identification**- Identify the problem at its core. Spend some time understanding the problem very clearly.

- **Objective**- The clearer the objective you want to achieve, the easier it will be to choose the right alternative.

- **Alternatives**- Don't make haste while exploring alternatives. **Be creative and jot down all the possible alternatives**, so you don't miss out on the best one.

- **Consequences- Identify the pros and cons of different alternatives. Go for the option that minimizes your risk and optimize your returns.**

- **Trade-offs**- Be mindful that by choosing one option out of many, you are ruling out the other options. **There is an opportunity cost involved in every decision. However, you have to be ready for trade-off between different options**. In complex decisions, there is no single perfect alternative. You have to choose intelligently among less-than perfect alternatives.

Use Ancient Intelligence: The **ancient intelligence that humans carry has the capability to put any behavior on autopilot** through the brain area known as basal ganglia. You can tap this ancient intelligence through the power of implementation intentions, or the **'if-then' technique**.

With this self-regulatory approach, you can program your mind in advance to take specific actions upon happening of specific conditions. This eliminates the need of making frequent and conscious decisions, as you have preset the algorithm of your mind to take predetermined actions based on the satisfaction of specific conditions. **You can train your brain with hundreds of such 'if-then' behaviors and put them on autopilot basis, thereby increasing your productivity 100,000 times.**

Chapter 7: How to Find Solutions Quickly around You

****

> *"Very often, when you change your perspective, you see things differently, make different decisions, and get different results."*
>
> *~Brian Tracy*

Not all decisions are equal. Some require extra diligence and care, because the consequence of mistakes can cost us dearly. When we face such decisions, we tend to get anxious: we think we might be missing something, or maybe we are not following the right sequence of steps. We start to think that our problem is unique and our life circumstances are peculiar and, therefore, no one else would be able to understand and guide us in the right direction.

This is a blatant irrational thought just popping up from anxious minds. Often, you can find the solution to your most pressing problem merely by just looking around in your surroundings. Let's look at some of the ways that will guide you towards instant solutions to our problems.

Solution Finders are Givers

Unless you are planning to launch a rocket to a planet (please ignore Mars because SpaceX founder, Elon Musk, has already indicated his plans to set up a human city there in the next few decades), chances are that people have already found the solution to your problem.

And here is the revelation.

There is a common trait in people who have found solutions. Their journey goes like this: first, they deeply immerse themselves to find the solution to the problem in such a way that they become almost invisible to others, because all great solutions require an intensity of focus. But once they find the solution, they can't help but stop themselves from giving the solution back to the world. Budhha left the world in his quest to answer why there is suffering in the world and how to end it. But when he became enlightened, he only returned to this world to spread his knowledge.

And this is not specific to any religious or spiritual belief; the concept of giving back appears everywhere. I was listening to an interview with Ray Dalio, the American billionaire (who we already talked about in a previous chapter). He stated that he has had a great amount of success throughout his entire life. He further explained that since he has turned 60 years, he doesn't want to focus his attention on adding more success to his own name; rather, **his new life purpose is to create a generation of successful young people**. He said that he is more than ready to provide the necessary guidance and support to the younger generation, so they can succeed.

Do you know why most high-achievers and successful people end up writing a book or getting their biographies done? Why do they do this? It's because their natural tendency is to give back to the world. As the saying goes, "Trees laden with fruits bow down." Am I sounding a bit preachy? Perhaps yes.

But my intent is only to show you that most problems of the world already have solutions. And the best part is that solution-finders want to spread their knowledge, so that people who are on the same path in their quest to find solutions don't suffer much and, instead, gain the wisdom to short-cut their process.

Of course, solution-finders won't come knocking at your door, offering you a gift-wrapped solution package. But it works pretty well the other way round – you go out, knock on their door, and chances are you'll find a solution. It depends on your level of commitment to find solution. As they say, "When the student is ready, the teacher will appear."

Therefore, don't worry. Most of the time, the solution is around you. Go out and look for the relevant books, courses, and, if needed, seek mentoring from the experts. Of course, there is a cost associated with everything, but sometimes the cost of not deciding or deciding wrongly is greater than investing in solutions. If you don't decide to invest a little sum, of course you'll save that small amount of money; but it will cost you more time and effort in learning from your own trial and error approach.

The hard reality is that unsuccessful people are spend time to save money, whereas successful people rather spend money to save time and rather multiply their time. And that's such an important distinction. Yes, because you can always get more money, but you can never get more time.

Gain from Your Competitors

Another strategy for finding solutions is to look at your competitors or people in the same domain as you are working in. Look at what they are doing.

Whenever you are thinking of venturing out with a new product or business, the best course of action is to look at what the competitors in that industry are already doing. If they are doing well, they must be doing certain things right. Your job is to track them down and see what they are doing right and start implementing these things into your business decisions.

There is a famous quote from Tony Robbins, ***"Success leaves clues."*** Of course, your competitors won't come and tell you their best strategies (they'd rather make the effort to keep them as secret); but if you are watchful, you can track their activities and find subtle cues and, thus, the best solution for your problem.

Let's take the real life example of Sam Walton, the founder of Walmart. In 1954, he took a 12-hour bus ride to see a new kind of checkout line at the Ben Franklin variety stores that led customers through one central line, rather than to separate counters for kitchen supplies, toiletries, groceries, etc. He was quite impressed by the solution and immediately implemented it in his own stores.

In fact, throughout his entire career, Walton kept an eye on what his competitors were doing better, even admitting that almost everything he'd ever done had been copied from someone else. That's why businesses spend so much time, money and effort getting market intelligence so they can save their own resources by applying the already researched and experimented tactics of their competitors to offer better solutions for their own consumer problems to grow faster.

Don't Ignore the Outside View -- Use Base Rates

It happens that we often give too much weight to some idea that we personally feel good about and get so obsessed with it that we ignore outside reality. We go with the solution we personally feel in our gut could shake the world, but we forget to see the trend or outside realities before investing too much in the idea.

I remember a real-life example when I was roaming around in a yet-to-be-fully-developed commercial area in my town. There were not many stores in operation yet, and I found new restaurant construction work going full swing. The owner was there, and I checked with him about the type of restaurant he was planning to start. As anyone would attend a prospective customer, the owner was forthcoming in telling me more about his upcoming restaurant. I asked him what his expectations and growth plans were. Becoming very excited, he cited the example of an upscale restaurant operating in a developed area of town, and he was very confident that as a result of his new venture, people would have a similar option available nearby, and they might just prefer his place.

I was intrigued. Although I didn't want to demoralize him, still I asked him why he thought that way, given that the market in the area was yet to be fully operational. But the young owner was too excited and energized and stated that the quality and experience he planned to give to his visitors would make his restaurant exceptional.

Later, when the restaurant opened, I made a few more visits to the area, but I didn't see any foodies or party goers flocking around. In about three to four months, I noticed that the restaurant had been shut down.

What was wrong with this young entrepreneur's decision? In fact, he had entirely ignored the outside view or the base rate of success before venturing out fully. Had he spent time analyzing the outside facts in the area and considered them in his decision making process, he might have revisited his decision to open restaurant in the first place. In reality, in that market, more than half of the shops that had opened were closed within a period of six months. The footfall of people was very low in the region to make any commercial sense for his restaurant. Probably, adjacent locals wanted to hang out in places where they could see a vibrant clientele and party-like environment, and this area lacked such a vibe.

That young entrepreneur simply assumed that merely because of the quality of his food and the ambience he provided, he would attract and retain high-quality customers. He ignored the outside reality. This leads me to one of the **most famous findings in the psychology of prediction -- the phenomenon of *"base rate neglect."***

Base rates means you need to assess the outside view of the goal you are targeting and the probability of achieving it. The real-world occurrence of instances gives you some probability of what to expect.

Your own instincts and gut feelings constitute the inside view of the situation from your own limited experience and perspective. But the actual results of the activities happening in real-life now or in the past make up the outside view. **The outside view gives you a base rate to guesstimate the probability of how much your results could vary**.

In the above example, the outside view of opening a restaurant or food joint in a newly-developing locality is not a good idea, because 50% of the new shops had shut down six months. There must have been a reason behind this massive failure rate, requiring analysis before making a decision. The young entrepreneur I described above neglected the base rate and simply went ahead in making a huge investment, solely relying on his own judgement and instincts.

However, this doesn't mean that you shouldn't trust your instincts or gut feelings; but at the same time, you should not entirely neglect the outside view or base rates of a particular situation.

How can you use this in real life?

When you approach experts about predicting a future situation, you should ask them base rate questions. This is because they also might be trapped in the inside view when presented with an individual situation; and they, too, might be neglecting base rates.

You should ask them _indicative_ rather than _predictive_ questions. For example, ask your lawyer about the percentage of cases like yours that have gained success in trials – this is the base rate question. You are asking for *indications* here. You'll get an outside view of the situation by asking such a question. However, if you simply ask whether your case will succeed in trial, it is **an inside view question**, and the answer you get might be ignorant of the base rates.

Now once you have taken a base rate view, even from the experts, you should examine your case closely to determine whether it is exactly like others, and, therefore, if you will meet the same fate, or you have figured out some unique aspects that will make your situation different.

Taking into account the outside along with inside view equips you with a holistic understanding of a situation, and, therefore, you can make smarter decisions.

Avoid Important Decisions in Stress Mode

As humans, we don't understand other people based merely on physical actions or verbal communication. Rather, we read faces and expressions and make judgments about what a person is thinking. For example, if your spouse or friend is upset with you and doesn't speak to you, you know something is wrong. You also understand non-verbal communication in the form of facial expressions: you can guess the mood of your manager.

But in the case of the disease called "autism," it cripples a person's ability to understand non-verbal communication. Afflicted people are blind to non-verbal signals: they only understand explicitly transmitted information and aren't able to read people's faces.

You might be wondering why am I telling you all this. It is because even non-autistic people can be rendered temporarily autistic, i.e., unable to understand non-verbal signals in stressful situations and under time pressure. When under stress, people tend to ignore many indirect signals like facial expressions and **go into *tunnel vision* mode**, devoting their entire attention to the most imminent "threat," meaning the most relevant piece of information.

Tunnel vision can, for example, cause police officers to shoot innocent people because they are focused so intently on the possible threat of a weapon such that even a black wallet can seem threatening like a gun.

If you want to avoid this kind of autistic "seizure," you have to slow down and reduce the stress in your environment. The worse the stress, the more likely you'll become temporarily autistic. And beyond a certain stress level, the logical thought process stops completely and people become very unpredictable.

Unless there are life threatening situations that triggers a fight or flight situation, you should not make important decisions when in stressful mode. In such situations, maybe drinking a glass of water and focusing on your breath for ten times, can relieve you from stress to some extent so you can avoid making wrong decisions influenced by stress.

Experiment New Ideas with Ooching

We are often faced with high-stake decisions in entirely new situations we are not aware of, and it's very difficult to predict the results of these decisions. In such situation, most people end up quitting the option altogether and become indecisive, because the stakes are really high and the results too unpredictable.

What should you do in such situations? There is a solution for this. You should use the process of testing the option on a smaller scale, known as "ooching." In such situations, it's wise to dip your toe in the water rather than dive in headfirst. Deciding upon something based on your *belief* that it will or won't work is a bad strategy compared to trying it on a smaller scale.

Take an example: undergoing an internship before venturing fully into a career is a really good idea because with minimal time and effort invested, you will know in less time whether you want to pursue that profession or not.

Moreover, we are bad about predicting our future, so instead of doing some guesswork, it is better to test it out on a smaller level to get a mini-version of what it will look like. I personally used this "ooching" experiment recently. I was about to enroll in an expensive coaching program, as I thought it would help me expedite my personal growth. But I was not fully convinced about the outcome. Therefore, I used this approach by enrolling in a low-cost mini-course with the same instructor. This approach helped me understand his methodology, style and content; and I was able to test it with a lower investment, and less time and effort before committing fully to the expensive program.

People often get stuck looking at the sheer volume of the activities involved in something and don't get started. They keep delaying taking action until they get the complete picture. But the ooching approach helps you get started at a smaller level, so you can review the mini-outcomes of your activities and enrich your experience in order to take up further challenges towards your bigger goals.

Chapter 7- Key Takeaways

We often think that to find solutions to our problems, we have to go to far off places to find experts who may not be available nearby. We tend to erroneously think that the solutions to our problem may not be available in the resources around us. But that's not entirely true for the following reasons:

- **Solution finders enjoy giving back**: People who arrive at a destination and become successful understand the pain of those who are starting out, so such people are ready to help, if approached correctly. **Moreover, you can find answers by reading books written by successful people or listening or watching them in**

interviews or on their social media. The best part is you don't need to physically go out, as you can easily find them in today's high-tech internet enabled smartphones and start seeking guidance from them immediately.

- **Gain insights from your competitors: You can learn a lot of good things from your competitors. If they are successful at doing something, then you need to closely watch them; and chances are that you'll find insights into some of the best practices that you can apply to your own operations. Success leaves clues, as Tony Robbins says, and you can follow those clues to attain success in your endeavors.**

- **Use base rates to improve decisions**: Following your gut or instincts is a good thing, but it doesn't have to be done in isolation. The best way is to see the general trend or base rates in similar situations and understand the results that other people are getting. **Follow your gut; but don't**

ignore the base rates entirely, and you'll avoid faulty decisions.

- **No decisions when in stress**: When your mind is clouded with stress, your cognitive faculties get engaged in thoughts that cause stress. In such a situation, you develop tunnel vision, as you are putting your entire thinking bandwidth on the situation causing stress. **In a stressful state, it's not possible to creatively think about more alternatives and analyze them properly, therefore avoid making significant decisions at this time.** Don't make key decisions in a state of stress. However, if you have to, then try to reduce stress immediately by focusing on your breathe or drinking some water.

- **Use ooching approach to test new ideas**: Don't make big decision about new things hastily. Don't start learning swimming directly in a deep river; rather, go for a low water level swimming pool. **However exciting or stimulating the idea of jumping all in might be, there**

are always certain nitty-gritty uncertainties about the situation that you don't know yet. Therefore, never test out a new idea by putting all your resources or energy into it; instead, follow the ooching approach. Wet your feet first, rather than diving in headfirst.

Chapter 8: 4 Simple Steps to Make Holistic Decisions

****

"It is in the moments of decision that our destiny is shaped."

– Tony Robbins

How to Make Holistic Decisions

Most people don't make decisions systematically; rather, they do it in a haphazard manner. There could be many reasons for this random approach. Most of the time, people realize that they are short of time and need to make fast decisions. Although they might have limited knowledge or understanding about the situation, they presume they have all the information or have an I-figured-it-all-out over-confidence that prompts them make decisions hastily.

Sometimes, people are just lazy and don't want to put even a minimal effort in finding relevant information for making effective decisions. In some cases, they don't know how to get more information by asking the right set of questions; and, therefore, they end up compromising with low-quality decision making.

Thus, most of the reasons for hasty, low-quality decisions generally can be put into a few categories, like a shortage of time, lack of information, over-confidence, and a lack of clarity on the right set of information required.

To address all of the above concerns, in this chapter, we will discuss one holistic decision-making method famously known as the WRAP method. As propounded by Chip and Dan Heath, academicians at Stanford University and Duke's University's CASE Center, respectively, this method is not some short-cut quick-fix kind of formula; rather it is a holistic approach to make better decisions.

The W.R.A.P. approach addresses all the important aspects related to effective decision making. The focus of the approach is to enable better decision making by focusing on often-ignored or overlooked factors that might have bigger ramifications in the long run in our lives.

W.R.A.P is acronym, as explained below, where each letter signifies a step-by-step approach to arrive at the best decision for a set of problems.

W- Widen your alternatives

R- Reality-test your assumptions

A- Attain Distance before making decisions

P- Prepare to be wrong

Let's expound upon each of these factors.

<u>Widen</u> Your Alternatives

We already discussed that people often tend to make decisions in a yes or no mode when confronted with making a choice. Assume you are a health-conscious person trying to stop eating junk fund. Suppose a friend asks you to order pizza. If you think of the answer in only yes or no, you are not going to be happy with any of your decisions. If you say yes, you'll feel guilty about eating the junk food, while if you say no, you'll feel sad about killing your desires.

You know already by now that you don't have to limit yourself to yes or no. Rather, you should go one level ahead and start exploring your options. You could ask what could other options exist from which you can choose? Maybe you can simply order a fresh salad from Subway -- adjacent to the pizza shop -- or go for healthy vegetable soup.

The first step in this process is all about widening your alternatives. It requires you to do some creative thinking. You need to be open to explore possibilities. Whether you're choosing food from a restaurant menu or are finalizing a destination for your next vacation, you need to explore the best possible alternatives. Whether you are applying for a new job and looking for the best companies to work for, or are launching a new product or service in the market, you should first think broadly about all the possibilities. Because you never know: a least probable option (at the stage of exploration) might turn out to be the best possible solution, once you research and analyze the possible outcomes, considering the given circumstances and other relevant factors.

Use Laddering Approach to Widen Your Alternatives

There is one wonderful approach for widening your options known as the **laddering approach**. Laddering is a staggered approach of broadening your exploration of alternatives. It suggests that whenever you need to make a decision about something, you need to start by looking *locally* in and around your own area. For example, if you want to open a restaurant in a particular locality, you would first look at current restaurants and the type of cuisine that is likely to have more demand. You then check out the numbers of Chinese, continental, Italian, or other cuisine restaurants. By looking at a variety of options, you broaden your understanding of the available options in the market.

The next step in the laddering approach is to go beyond the local and think **regionally**. Now you need to look around the whole area to see the restaurants that are running well. By thinking at the next region level, you'll find more options to help you decide better.

But you don't need to stop at the regional level. You can move ahead and explore the far distance, maybe look at what's happening **internationally**. This will broaden your thinking horizon about what's working well in other countries and how you can gain the first mover advantage by looking at the early trends.

I recall an approach suggested by Tony Robbins called, "***broadening the reference fabric***"-- meaning you need to enhance your understanding of the subject by exposing your mind to different types of reference points. With the enhanced reference fabric, your thinking horizon broadens, and you become more creative and generate better ideas. After all, most creativity is nothing but a fusion of different ideas taken from all kinds of places or people and coming out with your own unique one.

Take the example of Scott Adams, the famous cartoonist of the Dilbert series. He had an idea in his head to explore things in a funny way, but he didn't consider himself good as a stand-up comedian. While he soon realized that he had artistic abilities, he didn't see himself as an artist like Picasso. He loved to talk about meaningless conversations in the corporate environment with a bit of sarcasm but with an objective to convey a message for improving the quality of life of corporate employees. By exploring various options, Adams broadened his reference fabric, and then a magical "*idea-fusion*" happened. He came out with a funny, artistic cartoon series focusing on the office environment and its meaningless discussions. The Dilbert cartoon series was born, an altogether unique project that no one had done in the past. That's how widening your alternatives works to improve your creativity and present you with different alternatives.

Remember your best decisions will always come from one of your best alternatives. So, don't act hastily and ignore your best possible alternative.

Reality-test your Assumptions

People almost always behave in an autopilot mode. They have their own assumptions about things, and they get influenced by these assumptions, so they end up making low-quality, ineffective decisions.

As you have already learned, we unconsciously act under the influence of the confirmation bias, which means we always try to find evidence that proves our beliefs to be true. It so happens that when someone is presenting a new or different idea, we tend to reject any new idea outright that doesn't match our existing beliefs.

We tend to justify our reasons by giving one or another argument like, "This product or service won't work in my city or town", or "I've not seen any such thing in my whole experience, so it's not a good idea to explore", or other such arguments. You try to assign as many reasons as you can to confirm your bias towards a particular view. Warren Buffet puts it very aptly, *"What the human being is best at doing is interpreting all new information so that their prior conclusions remain intact."*

Precisely, our assumptions about various things, people and events are strongly influenced by the confirmation bias. This requires sincere work to counter those self-imposed limitations in our thinking. Here are a few helpful approaches to reality test your assumption about alternatives, before you make a conclusive decision.

> a. ***Use critical thinking***: *Start by asking a discomforting question, one that goes against your preconceived notions or pre-set beliefs. If you decide based on an old assumption that things will continue to work in a particular way, you need to ask tough questions like, "Is there a possibility that you will get laid off or fired from the job you consider a safe*

haven, and what would be the reasons? or "what if market dynamics catapult and you end up sitting with obsolete products or unwanted service offerings?"

This approach is also known as black hat thinking, one of the six thinking approaches suggested by Edward De Bono in his best seller book, *Six Thinking Hats*. **The approach requires you to critically examine everything that can go wrong about your decisions** and then carefully assess different alternative based on your most important parameters. Critical thinking prepares you to handle the worst case scenarios and triggers your imagination to foresee and examine various alternatives.

b. *Zoom out- This approach requires closely looking at the finer details of a situation by getting into the nuts and bolts of each alternative. You need to closely examine the various aspects or activities involved in your preferred alternative and the level of knowledge or skill sets required to handle them. This approach intends to rule out any alternative, where due to a missing link or some key technical requirement, a higher cost, or any other requirements, you might end up losing financially and emotionally.*

c. **Take baby steps**- *Use the ooching approach you have learned already and get your feet wet before you jump fully into the water. Why rely on your prediction when you can see the results of your preferred alternative in a smaller version? You already know that ooching takes the guesswork out of the job and helps you directly experience the pros and cons of your best alternative.*

d. *You can do a reality test of your assumption* **by taking the outside or base rate view**, *as discussed. This requires you to examine the situation from the outside by taking a holistic or bigger picture view. Whatever alternative you're thinking of, you can do research on the outcome of the decisions taken by people in similar situations. Remember the example of opening a restaurant in a high-street traffic area; you need to check the actual success rate of* *the restaurants in that area and take it into consideration before you make decisions.*

Attain Distance

Can you see your own glasses when you have them on? No, because you see through them only. Only a person from the outside can tell you how your glasses look (unless you remove them and see them on your own).

How is this example relevant here? It means you cannot see something objectively when you are closely associated with it. It is the same when we are too closely attached to your ideas. You love your ideas like your own babies – and, therefore, they always sound like the best ones. And no one loves to find or accept fault in their own babies?

We remain stuck in the status quo, because we don't step back to see things from a distance. But when reviewing an alternative, it is of the utmost necessity to somehow create a distance from your own thinking.

How do you create a distance? **It's by shifting your perspective.** You can look at your problem as a friend's problem, and not yours. This immediately helps you see it outside of your head. Now you need to analyze what would you advise your friend to do in a similar situation.

Often, we are clouded by our own circumstances and prejudices when making decisions for ourselves. But when we need to advise our friends, we become more objective. You might remember the example from a previous chapter, where you chose to advise your friend to go to his or her boss to clarify a situation (you took an independent view here), but if you were to take similar action in a situation applicable to you, you would find yourself influenced by the emotions of fear, anxiety or "what-will-he-say-or-think?" kind of thoughts. Bestselling author and speaker, John. C. Maxwell, puts into apt words, ***"One of the reasons that problem solving is so difficult is that we are often too close to the problems to truly understand them."***

Shifting your perspective about alternatives provides you with an altogether different and maybe better alternative. Let me tell you a real-life story that shows the huge benefit of shifting one's perspective in problem solving.

Mike Abrashoff was the captain of a ship named, the USS Benefold, which became one of the best ships in the United States Navy under his captaincy. **The staff under his leadership was committed to challenge the *status quo* in every area**. I'll now share one specific instance where looking at a situation by attaining distance provided a major shift in perspective and saved time, effort and lots of money.

Here was the brilliant idea. The ship was required to be painted every month, necessitating around one month's time to cover the entire vessel. This painting was necessary because rust stains mar the finish and run down the sides. One sailor suggested to Abrashoff that swapping the ferrous metal fasteners (nuts, bolts, etc.) topside with stainless steel (which doesn't rust in salt water) would eliminate a lot of repetitive work. It was a no-brainer, but no one had ever thought about it from a different perspective. Abrashoff adopted the idea and the ship not only went ten months between paintings, but the entire Navy adopted the program. Every ship now uses a stainless steel topside – saving millions of dollars – all because there was a shift in perspective in looking at familiar things.

Prepare to be Wrong

The last string of the WRAP approach is about being prepared to be wrong. We often get started with a new project often being over-confident, thinking our decisions will turn out to be right; but the hard reality is that we don't' know what is in future and how it will unfold.

The approach of always thinking that our decisions will turn out the way we want inhibits are desire to explore the negative aspects of the decision-making process. There is a different approach that requires us to be prepared for bad outcomes called ***pre-mortem***. Pre-mortem is a managerial strategy in which a project team imagines that a project has failed and then works backwards to see what potentially could lead to the failure of other projects.

A 2007 article from the Harvard Business Review states that unlike a typical critiquing session, in which project team members are asked what *might* go wrong, **the pre-mortem approach operates on the assumption that the "patient" has died, and so asks what *did* go wrong.**

This is the imagination of a worst case scenario and then thinking backwards about the reasons for the failure and what you could have done to address what led to it. Moreover, if you are prepared to be wrong in any situation, it allows you to make alternative plans with which you can transition. This approach can provide you with many reasons that hypothetically could be leading to failure. The approach therefore equips you to work cautiously on everything that could bring about a bad outcome.

If things don't go the way you thought despite being cautious about possible pitfalls, preparing to be wrong helps you to devise backup plans. You would prepare Plan B or Plan C if your key Plan A doesn't succeed. This will help you transition smoothly to alternative plans.

All in all, if you are prepared in advance to be wrong, you'll be able to control the situation more easily than when you haven't taken into account the untoward scenario.

To sum up, the WRAP Formula empowers you with a vast number of alternatives to choose from. It warns you to do a realty test of the situation with wide open eyes, shift your perspective to see alternatives objectively, and finally be fully prepared if things don't go the way you thought.

Therefore, the WRAP formula helps you take a holistic view of a situation and make a decision that shows the full utilization of your cognitive abilities and instincts. This approach helps you deconstruct complex problems holistically into well-examined alternatives, thus enabling you to make smarter decisions in every situation.

Chapter 8- Key Takeaways

This four step formula is a perfect way to holistically analyze a problem and possible solutions in case of complex situations. Here are the steps.

- **Widen your alternatives**: Use your imagination, think creatively and widen the net of possible solutions to any problem. You can follow the laddering approach, whereby you broaden your alternatives in a staggered manner. Therefore, the very first step is to equip yourself with all the possible solutions for the problem to which you are seeking a solution.

- **Reality-test your assumption**: You may have preconceived notions or assumptions about an alternative that may not be entirely true; rather, it could be your myopic view or a subjective opinion about the situation. Therefore, to make the best holistic decision, always be open to objectively testing your options based on ground reality. You should think critically, zoom into each alternative and go deeper into all the aspects. Then test it out by taking some baby steps to reality assess all your assumption. This will give you an objective perspective of every situation and help you take an unbiased view.

- **Attain distance from your ideas**: To objectively assess your ideas, you need to create some distance from your own thinking process. You have to look at them objectively from an independent person's perspective. This is because once you think about your ideas in for a long time, you form a specific perspective about them. Taking a distance from the problem or situation enables you to shift perspectives. **Only with a renewed perspective can objectively see through to other elements that are generally missed.** This approach will help you to have a holistic perspective and make better decisions.

- **Prepare to be wrong**: Use the pre-mortem technique. Assume that the decision you have taken has already gone wrong and now you are analyzing the reasons why. **The pre-mortem technique helps you list all the possible causes that could have led to the bad decision.** Once you have a list of all those causes or reasons that led to failure in your imaginary situation, **you can now plan a the** activities that need to be done to avoid committing those mistakes.

Chapter 9: How to Approach Your Future as your Most Trusted Guide

****

"If you work hard enough and assert yourself, and use your mind and imagination, you can shape the world to your desires."

— Malcolm Gladwell

The decisions of today define the trajectory of one's life and determine how the future will turn out tomorrow.

Life is much like a game of golf. When you have taken a position to hit the ball with your club, you need to be extra cautious about the direction in addition to the amount of force you apply. Even if you hit the ball with the right force, a mere two degrees of deviation can land the ball a few hundred meters from the hole.

The same principle applies to life decisions as well. Even a minor deviation or error in your decisions can have a major impact, taking your life in an altogether different direction. How minor errors can lead to a major disaster in life was proven by an accident that took hundreds of lives. In the late 1970s, a New Zealand airline used to fly from New Zealand for sightseeing over Antarctica and would return back in the evening of the same day. On one tragic day in November of 1979, a flight was carrying more than 200 passengers. Accidently, the coordinates of the flight path were pre-set incorrectly by a mere two degrees one night before the next morning's flight and, unfortunately, the crew was not informed of it.

The plane started out normally on its way to Antarctica, but instead of going in the right direction, it was re-routed in the path of a mountain. By the time the crew members realized the error, it was too late. They couldn't correct the route of the flight at the last moment and all the passengers died in that tragic accident.

The above example shows how future outcomes are dependent on the right decisions we take today. Therefore, doesn't it make sense to put the future scenario in your mind before deciding anything?

Yes, absolutely. In fact, we should think about how the future could be altered by making different choices today. Let's now understand a few resourceful approaches that will prompt you to keep future outcomes in mind first and foremost when making any decision.

Follow the 10/10/10 Rule

This rule is pretty straightforward. Before making any big decision in your life, ask yourself how that decision will affect you in the next 10 minutes, the next 10 months, and the next 10 years.

Most of the time, our tendency is to make decisions based on our short-term emotions. We feel that we need a product or service right now. Have you ever wondered why you make impulse decisions? **It's because *your present emotions are very clear and precise, while future emotions are not yet well defined***. Smart salespersons exploit this human tendency to sell more of their products or services. They try to excite us based on that short-term present emotion to influence our decisions. Promotional messages are crafted to trigger instant emotions and unconsciously force us to make an unplanned decision to buy a product – something known as impulse buying (of course, later you regret making that decision).

Here comes the 10/10/10 rule to empower you and equalize the impact of this short-term influence on your emotions. What this rule recommends is whenever you are faced with decision problems, you need to actively think about what your future emotions would be like, if you choose to make the decision. **You can awaken your future emotions by asking yourself how would you feel about your decision in *10 minutes, 10 months,* or *10 years* from the moment of making it.**

It helps if the future emotions that arise while thinking about the short- and long-term picture sound equally clear, precise, and supportive of your objective. Only then should you decide to go ahead with the alternative.

Take this example. Assume you have two alternatives: either a subscription for video game app for 3 months or a period of one year. Obviously, to get the benefit of your current emotions, the video gaming company is offering you a one-year subscription at more than 50% off the regular rate. Your emotions will focus on the huge saving of 50% by going for a one-year subscription.

But if you think from the 10/10/10 perspective and take the future perspective, you will soon realize that taking a one-year plan will make you more addicted to video game playing. Although you are saving money currently, in 10 months or 10 years from the moment of decision, you could be enslaved to an unhealthy habit. With that realization, you will think of an alternate option. Remember the earlier case: "keep the $14.99 for other purchases" as an example of decision making in a previous chapter. If you think about other options, you can simply replace a habit with a gym membership - a healthier alternative. It boils down to the fact that spending some amount of time checking your emotions by considering the future scenario empowers you to make more beneficial decisions for yourself.

Use Prospective Hindsight

We often imagine one possible consequence of our actions and base our decisions on that one specific idea of how the future will unfold, despite the fact that we have no way of actually predicting the future.

In reality, we can only make a prediction of the future based on the limited information we have. But the future can throw us many new, unknown, and uncertain curves that we probably have not yet experienced in our lives. At this stage, we find ourselves standing at a crossroad - while we have to make a decision, we have a very limited amount of information to make a prediction of the future outcome.

Although we learned the 40:70 R\rule in a previous chapter that addresses making decisions when you have a limited amount of information, there is another approach that will guide you to take the right action in the present moment to avoid a future disaster.

It is a technique called Prospective Hindsight that can help improve one's future vision. **The word "prospective" means to imagine a scenario, and the word *hindsight* means to look back from the scenario to the cause of it**. This technique is somewhat similar (just slightly different, as explained below) to *project pre-mortem*.

Let's understand how this works. As humans, we are not that good at evaluating future possibilities compared to actual facts. We can easily post-mortem a fact and find the reasons for it by constructing an anatomy of the situation. But, unfortunately, we can't do it with the same level of precision in the case of a future possibility.

The prospective hindsight philosophy helps you hypothetically go into the future and ask yourself a question, *"It's one year from now and the project I started has failed, why?"* rather than, *"What could be the reasons that led to future failure?"*

The prospective hindsight approach helps you think broadly about the possible reasons for failure, and once you list those reasons, you'll find yourself better equipped to look at options that could prevent it.

Here is how this technique is different from the pre-mortem approach we talked about earlier. In fact, prospective

hindsight is not merely thinking about a future disaster scenario. You can imagine a more positive scenario of glorious success. Think of what has led to your success and then improve on those factors. Use this approach to ensure you're able to handle any possible success. For example, if you plan to launch a new product, do you have the capability of meeting demand should it suddenly become successful and popular? Do you have the proper infrastructure in place to produce and distribute your products, if demand explodes? You should also implement a safety factor to be prepared for unforeseeable circumstances.

Consider the example of the strength of ropes in an elevator: the cables are eleven times stronger than needed to function. Engineers calculate how much weight it will transport, what strain will be put on the cables, and which will carry that weight. Then, they multiply the answer by eleven. Similarly, when engineers construct a bridge, they design it in such a way to take the load of multiple times than what has been sanctioned, so it can handle any unforeseen circumstances.

We tend to be overconfident in our knowledge, so it's a good idea to be rather cautious and adjust your predictions based on that fact. The prospective hindsight technique works by using a human's ability to analyze actual facts. By imagining future events as actual fact, we are better able to determine the reason for failure or success, helping us to expand our thinking horizon so we can make more informed and better decisions.

To conclude, the techniques stated in this chapter will help you get the benefit of your future emotions and the human brain's capabilities to look at future events as actual facts. All the decisions we make today are made in order to get better results and feel good about those decisions in the future.

Therefore, the methods stated in this chapter will help you see yourself standing in the future, as a result of the decisions taken today; and this helps you make decisions more confidently.

Chapter 9- Key Takeaways

While making decisions, you should take into account the possible impact of your choices on your future. If you do so, your future will become your best guide and direct you whether to make a particular decisions or pass on them this time.

- **Follow the 10/10/10 rule**: Your present emotions are precise, while, on the other hand, your future emotions are not yet well defined.

Unfortunately, most decisions are based on short-term emotions, and we don't take into account the future emotions that we would feel based on the outcome we get. **Therefore, you need to activate your future emotions by asking yourself how you would feel about your decision in *10 minutes*, *10 months*, or *10 years* from the moment of making the decision.** When you know how you would feel in the future for decisions taken based on today's emotions, it will impact the quality of these decisions in the present moment.

- **Use prospective hindsight**: While it is difficult to assess the future outcome of any decision, it is comparatively easy to assess the reasons for an event that has already occurred. With prospective hindsight, you hypothetically see yourself in a future situation where your decision has already gone wrong. **Then you question yourself about the reasons that led to the failure; and with that list of reasons, you will find yourself wiser and not likely to commit those mistakes**.

Similarly, with prospective hindsight, you can imagine getting a positive outcome from your decisions, analyze the reasons behind this hypothetical success and then use it to narrow down your efforts to aspects that deliver better results. This will also prepare you to handle the large amount of activities arising from the success of your project.

Final Thoughts

****

"Nothing happens until you decide. Make a decision and watch your life move forward."

--Oprah Winfrey

Congratulations! You made it to the end in this running-like-mad world where people often quit every another project they start.

I believe you must have gotten a few nuggets of wisdom from this book, so that you can start implementing them in your life.

In fact, you don't have to wait for some big project to start applying the techniques learned in this book. You are making decisions every moment of your life, so you can start with any of the choices you want to make right now and begin applying the stated principles.

Peter Drucker, a famous management consultant, rightly stated: ***"Making good decisions is a crucial skill at every level."***

Decision making is, and will always remain, a highly-in-demand cognitive skill. Like any other skill, you can develop it with consistent practice. You need to set your own false and limiting presumptions aside and expand your thinking horizon. You can start by questioning your existing cognitive biases by applying critical thinking and using your creativity and imagination to expand the number of alternatives in any area of decision making.

Don't let the fear of failure hinder you from taking action. Remember this quote from Maimonides, a Jewish philosopher, who said, ***"The risk of a wrong decision is preferable to the terror of indecision."***

Now at the end, I urge you to start using these principles in your day-to-day life. Keep refreshing these principles by consistently implementing them in both your small and big decisions, and very soon, you'll find yourself making decisions more confidently and taking full charge of your life.

I wish you nothing but grand success.

Cheers

Som Bathla

May I ask you for a small favor?

At the outset, I want to give you a big thanks for taking out time to read this book. You could have chosen any other book, but you took mine, and I totally appreciate this.

I hope you got at least a few actionable insights that will have a positive impact on your day to day life.

Can I ask for 30 seconds more of your time?

I'd love if you could leave a review about the book. Reviews may not matter to big-name authors; but they're a tremendous help for authors like me, who don't have much following. They help me to grow my readership by encouraging folks to take a chance on my books.

To put it straight– **reviews are the life blood for any author.**

Please leave your review by clicking below will directly lead you to book review page.

CLICK TO LEAVE YOUR REVIEW HERE

It will just take less than a minute of yours, but will tremendously help me to reach out to more people, so please leave your review.

Thanks for your support to my work. And I'd love to see your review.

Full Book Summary

Introduction- Key Takeaways

Every moment of your life requires you to make some kind of decision. It could be a small miniature choice or a life-altering decision.

Even if you don't decide on any particular situation, you unconsciously made a choice to not decide on that matter.

Not doing anything and just waiting to see what happens in the future is nothing but a decision to not improve and adapt yourself to today's dynamic and ever-changing world, thus becoming obsolete and easily replaceable by those who consistently change.

Chapter 1- Key Takeaways

Making a decision is about "cutting off" choices — cutting off other courses of action and coming out with a final choice among many.

The two biggest challenges in decision making are:

1. **Information Overload**: As per Miller's Law, the human brain can process seven (+/- two) chunks of information at a time. But in today's information age, with the ease of information dissemination and vast outreach of social media, you are overexposed to information. This leads to **information overload because the amount of input to your brain's cognitive faculties far exceeds its processing capacity.**

Information overload also cause to "filter failure" for your brain, meaning you are unable to filter the relevant and important information from the irrelevant and insignificant details.

2. **Paralysis by Analysis**: This occurs when you start to overthink and overanalyze any situation and the available alternatives to resolve a given problem. This causes more harm than good, as you replace action with idle thinking and don't make any decision -- leading to indecision.

Moreover, in more complex situations, there are few other challenges that one needs to understand:

- Uncertainty of the situation in the future
- Complexity due to multiple factors
- Consequences that have high stakes
- Availability of numerous alternatives

Interpersonal issues where other persons are affected and thus need to be involved in the decision-making process

Chapter 2- Key Takeaways

It's not only the outside factors that make decision making difficult, but there are many internal hidden traps that trip us and lead to bad choices:

- **Anchoring Trap: Our minds are influenced by the first set of alternatives, and this colors all other future alternatives.** Any marketer would offer you an initial price of 97$, before discounting it and finally selling it to you for 27$, because the anchoring trap makes you believe that you are getting 97$ worth value for just 27$. So beware of this trap.

- **Status Quo Trap**: Human beings love certainty and the security of the future. For most people, trying something new means uncertainty, discomfort, and risk; therefore, **maintaining the status quo is their natural reaction.**

- **Sunk Cost Trap**: After making a wrong decision, people often continue with it for a much longer time, instead of correcting it. Changing the course of action causes a big dent in one's ego, as it implies that we made the wrong decision earlier, and that's not easy to accept for most. Moreover, if it has huge consequences, people avoid admitting to their mistakes and continue with the hope that the situation will improve.

- **Confirmation Evidence Trap**: When we have an existing belief about something, we don't want to listen to an alternate view; rather, we try to find evidence that support our pre-existing belief. Due to this trap, we don't try newer things and explore better opportunities, because we are **more focused on proving ourselves right, rather than choosing something that's actually right.**

- **Framing Trap:** Our ability to respond to any situation is strongly influenced by the way the situation is framed. If the framing shows a bigger advantage or pleasure or avoids some big pain or problem, we are immediately inclined to make a decision, as compared to situations that are framed in a way that is not very clear or precise, or does not evoke emotions.

- **Recallability Trap**: We are influenced more by the recency of events and those situations that we can recall immediately. This leads to **assigning undue weight to current situations and all but ignoring events or situations we don't recollect** – meaning we don't take into account the insights gained from our distant past and, thus, make faulty decisions.

Chapter 3- Key Takeaways

The quality and speed of your decisions will depend on the end objective behind any decision. Based on the end objective approach, we can categorize decision makers into four different types of archetypes:

- **Maximizer**: They are thorough researchers and explore the best possible alternatives to arrive at a decision; but, sadly, despite arriving at the best decision, they start fretting about, if they come across some other better alternative. **They want to maximize their results all the time, so every new shiny object can easily make them unhappy and dissatisfied** – NOT a good archetype to be.

- **Satisficer**: Satisficers first decide their parameters and standards for making decision- and these standards can be high. They look for alternative based on their parameter requirements, and once an alternative meets their requirement, they make a decision. **The best part is, once they make a decision, they are satisfied and don't get disturbed by another better alternatives**, unless the prior choice fails to meet their standards or they evolve and eventually improve their standard. **This is a better approach to decision making that allows you to stay happy and contented with your decision.**

- **Perfectionist**: They set standards that are too high and even they themselves don't expect to meet.

Always straining for making flawless choices and affected by others' opinions on these choices, they take on stress compulsively toward unattainable goals and measure their self-worth by productivity and accomplishment. **They end up not making any decisions because they can't achieve perfection; they can only strive for it. Avoid this trap, because "done is way better than perfect."**

- **Optimalist**: This is the best archetype one should strive for. Optimalists are considerate of the hard core realities of what is achievable and what is not. They know what is controllable and what is not. They know that things can't be perfect, so they choose to strive for perfection; but they won't face regret like Maximizers or Perfectionists. **They are not maniac Maximizers (always running behind next shiny objects). Rather, they are ambitious Satisficers (setting ever higher stretchable standards and striving to attain them).**

Chapter 4- Key Takeaways

Humans wrongly believe themselves to be rational beings, while truth is most of our decisions are influenced by pre-existing beliefs formed based on our life circumstances, past experiences and emotional state when making decisions.

Many techniques help us avoid making faulty decisions:

- **Be aware of unconscious association**: Our unconscious associations about our own identity or that of other persons formed on the basis of surrounding environment or past experiences influences our behavior and actions when making different decisions. **The best solution to overcome this to become aware of such associations.** This awareness comes from asking questions about different unconscious assumptions. Merely awareness of these associations can significantly improve our decision-making.

- **Handle the liking and mirroring Bias**: Marketers tend to influence our buying decisions by flattering or mirroring our gestures, as everyone loves to be praised and liked. **To avoid being manipulated and take the right decisions, you should be more watchful of such behavior** and if needed, seek guidance from someone who is independent and has not any vested interest in the offer.

- **Use the observer perspective**: You may often be quick to give advice to others in different situations, if you are not emotionally involved in their situations. However, when you have to make your own decisions in similar situations, it's difficult to follow that advice. **The best solution here is to disengage yourself from your situation and look at it from an observer's perspective** to get an objective and independent view of the situation.

- **How to shift from autopilot to manual behavior**: Humans are creatures of habit and routine; followed for a long time, it becomes autopilot like brushing your teeth. **To avoid making decisions on**

an autopilot basis, you need to give a tripwire or shock to your mind – anything that forces you think differently and trigger different behavior.

- **Change behavior with deadlines/partitions**. Offering deadlines to a particular activity or assigning a series of milestones to any major goal is a perfect strategy to stay alert and come out of autopilot behavior.

Chapter 5- Key Takeaways

You really don't need that much quantity of information; rather, you need right quality of information. Here is how to do it.

- **Don't always decide in yes or no**: Deciding always in yes or no is not the best approach, as it sometimes puts you in a stressful situation. Therefore, **instead of agreeing or disagreeing, try to explore other alternatives or possibilities**. When you demand yourself to think beyond yes or no options, you'll generate a few other alternatives to mull over. Once you have other options besides the one presented to you, compare them, and whatever gives the best return for your time and attention, go for it. **Always ask yourself, "Is there any other option?"**

Your time, energy and efforts are limited resources, and there is opportunity cost for not choosing a particular alternative. Therefore, generate more alternatives beyond simple "yes" or "no" and go for the best one.

- **Multi-tracking of information**: Instead of working on one option to solve a problem, the better approach is to work simultaneously on other alternatives. **"Multi-tracking of information"** offers you the benefit of exploring the pros and cons of several options simultaneously. If one option doesn't seem to work, you can immediately switch to another option or produce a combination of the best out of multiple choices. **This sharpens your cognitive abilities, as you will make fine distinctions between different options** by practically working on them simultaneously.

- **Avoid choice overload**: Don't over burden yourself with too many choices. Research shows that the more the number of options, the more difficult it becomes to make decisions. The paradox of choice will overwhelm you, and you'll tend to procrastinate and not take further action.

Please bear in mind that you don't have to always choose between yes or no. It's always recommended to enhance the number of options and follow multi-tracking of information, but you have to be cautious to limit the number of your choices, so you are not plagued by the paradox of choice.

- **Avoid irrelevant information**: Humans have a short attention span, so you need to be wise when exposing yourself to information and eliminate irrelevant stuff. **Avoid decision fatigue** by not wasting your willpower on routine decisions like choosing meals or clothes, and keep it reserved for important issues. **Use the "Elimination by**

Aspects Model" and evaluate each piece of available information through the lens of a pre-identified set of parameters based on importance.

If any piece of information doesn't meet important parameters, it needs to be eliminated quickly, and one should focus only on relevant information to speed up the decision making process.

- **Follow the 40:70 rule**: You don't need to wait for 100% of the information to make decisions. **Follow Collin Powell's Rule – if you have information of more than 40% and up to 70% for making any particular decision, don't wait and just make the decision**. There will always be an element of uncertainty in every situation. Waiting until all the uncertainties are crystal clear is a perfectionist tendency, because situations can never be "perfect". Therefore, follow Collin Powell's 40-70% rule and make start making decisions based on your judgement of the limited set of information available.

Chapter 6- Key Takeaways

Before you make any decision, you must understand the key elements of each decision. Effective decision making is focused on:

- *what's important to you*
- *It should be logical and consistent*
- It should be *holistic* and takes into all elements
- *It encourages gathering as much relevant information as necessary*

Follow the PrOACT Approach: PrOACT is an acronym, where each character explains the process of effective decision making as below:

- **Problem Identification**- Identify the problem at its core. Spend some time understanding the problem very clearly.

- **Objective**- The clearer the objective you want to achieve, the easier it will be to choose the right alternative.

- **Alternatives**- Don't make haste while exploring alternatives. **Be creative and jot down all the possible alternatives**, so you don't miss out on the best one.

- **Consequences**- Identify the pros and cons of different alternatives. Go for the option that minimizes your risk and optimize your returns.

- **Trade-offs**- Be mindful that by choosing one option out of many, you are ruling out the other options. **There is an opportunity cost involved in every decision. However, you have to be ready for trade-off between different options**. In complex decisions, there is no single perfect alternative. You have to choose intelligently among less-than perfect alternatives.

Use Ancient Intelligence: The **ancient intelligence that humans carry has the capability to put any behavior on autopilot** through the brain area known as basal ganglia. You can tap this ancient intelligence through the power of implementation intentions, or the **'if-then' technique**.

With this self-regulatory approach, you can program your mind in advance to take specific actions upon happening of specific conditions. This eliminates the need of making frequent and conscious decisions, as you have preset the algorithm of your mind to take predetermined actions based on the satisfaction of specific conditions. **You can train your brain with hundreds of such 'if-then' behaviors and put them on autopilot basis, thereby increasing your productivity 100,000 times.**

Chapter 7- Key Takeaways

We often think that to find solutions to our problems, we have to go to far off places to find experts who may not be available nearby. We tend to erroneously think that the solutions to our problem may not be available in the resources around us. But that's not entirely true for the following reasons:

- **Solution finders enjoy giving back**: People who arrive at a destination and become successful understand the pain of those who are starting out, so such people are ready to help, if approached correctly. **Moreover, you can find answers by reading books written by successful people or listening or watching them in interviews or on their social media.** The best part is you don't need to physically go out, as you can easily find them in today's high-tech internet enabled smartphones and start seeking guidance from them immediately.

- **Gain insights from your competitors:** You can learn a lot of good things from your competitors. **If they are successful at doing something, then you need to closely watch them; and chances are that you'll find insights into some of the best practices that you can apply to your own operations. Success leaves clues, as Tony Robbins says, and you can follow those clues to attain success in your endeavors.**

- **Use base rates to improve decisions**: Following your gut or instincts is a good thing, but it doesn't have to be done in isolation. The best way is to see the general trend or base rates in similar situations and understand the results that other people are getting. **Follow your gut; but don't ignore the base rates entirely, and you'll avoid faulty decisions**.

- **No decisions when in stress**: When your mind is clouded with stress, your cognitive faculties get engaged in thoughts that cause stress. In such a situation, you develop tunnel vision, as you are putting your entire thinking bandwidth on the situation causing stress. **In a stressful state, it's not possible to creatively think about more alternatives and analyze them properly, therefore avoid making significant decisions at this time**. Don't make key decisions in a state of stress. However, if you have to, then try to reduce stress immediately by focusing on your breathe or drinking some water.

- **Use the ooching approach to test new ideas**: Don't make big decision about new things hastily. Don't start learning swimming directly in a deep river; rather, go for a low water level swimming pool. **However exciting or stimulating the idea of jumping all in might be, there are always certain nitty-gritty uncertainties about the situation that you don't know**

yet. Therefore, never test out a new idea by putting all your resources or energy into it; instead, follow the ooching approach. Wet your feet first, rather than diving in headfirst.

Chapter 8- Key Takeaways

This four step formula is a perfect way to holistically analyze a problem and possible solutions in case of complex situations. Here are the steps.

- **Widen your alternatives**: Use your imagination, think creatively and widen the net of possible solutions to any problem. You can follow the laddering approach, whereby you broaden your alternatives in a staggered manner. Therefore, the very first step is to equip yourself with all the possible solutions for the problem to which you are seeking a solution.

- **Reality-test your assumption**: You may have preconceived notions or assumptions about an alternative that may not be entirely true; rather, it could be your myopic view or a subjective opinion about the situation. Therefore, to make the best holistic decision, always be open to objectively testing your options based on ground reality. You should think critically, zoom into each alternative and go deeper into all the aspects. Then test it out by taking some baby steps to reality assess all your assumption. This will give you an objective perspective of every situation and help you take an unbiased view.

- **Attain distance from your ideas**: To objectively assess your ideas, you need to create some distance from your own thinking process. You have to look at them objectively from an independent person's perspective. This is because once you think about your ideas in for a long time, you form a specific perspective about them. Taking a distance from the problem or situation enables you to shift perspectives. **Only with a renewed perspective can objectively see through to other elements that are generally missed.** This approach will help you to have a holistic perspective and make better decisions.

- **Prepare to be wrong**: Use the pre-mortem technique. Assume that the decision you have taken has already gone wrong and now you are analyzing the reasons why. **The pre-mortem technique helps you list all the possible causes that could have led to the bad decision.** Once you have a list of all those causes or reasons that led to failure in your imaginary situation, **you can now plan a the activities that need to be done to avoid committing those mistakes**.

Chapter 9- Key Takeaways

While making decisions, you should take into account the possible impact of your choices on your future. If you do so, your future will become your best guide and direct you whether to make a particular decisions or pass on them this time.

- **Follow the 10/10/10 rule**: Your present emotions are precise, while, on the other hand, your future emotions are not yet well defined. Unfortunately, most decisions are based on short-term emotions, and we don't take into account the future emotions that we would feel based on the outcome we get. **Therefore, you need to activate your future emotions by asking yourself how you would feel about your decision in *10 minutes, 10 months, or 10 years* from the moment of making the decision.** When you know how you would feel in the future for decisions taken based on today's emotions, it will impact the quality of these decisions in the present moment.

- **Use prospective hindsight**: While it is difficult to assess the future outcome of any decision, it is comparatively easy to assess the reasons for an event that has already occurred. With prospective hindsight, you hypothetically see yourself in a future situation where your decision has already gone wrong. **Then you question yourself about the reasons that led to the failure; and with that list of reasons, you will find yourself wiser and not likely to commit those mistakes**. Similarly, with prospective hindsight, you can imagine getting a positive outcome from your decisions, analyze the reasons behind this hypothetical success and then use it to narrow down your efforts to aspects that deliver better results. This will also prepare you to handle the large amount of activities arising from the success of your project.

Could you please leave a review on the book?

One last time!

I'd love if you could leave a review about the book. Reviews may not matter to big-name authors; but they're a tremendous help for authors like me, who don't have much following. They help me to grow my readership by encouraging folks to take a chance on my books.

To put it straight– **reviews are the life blood for any author.**

Please leave your review by clicking below will directly lead you to book review page.

CLICK TO LEAVE YOUR REVIEW HERE

It will just take less than a minute of yours, but will tremendously help me to reach out to more people, so please leave your review.

Thank you for supporting my work and I'd love to see your review soon

Preview of the book "Build a Happier Brain"

Introduction

****

> *"When I was five years old, my mother always told me that happiness was the key to life. When I went to school, they asked me what I wanted to be when I grew up. I wrote down 'happy'. They told me I didn't understand the assignment, <u>and I told them they didn't understand life.</u>"*
>
> *~John Lennon, Singer, Founder of Beatles*

Happiness Requires a 'Shift' in Thinking

A group of around fifty people was attending a conference. Suddenly, the speaker stopped and decided to do a group activity; he gave each person a balloon. The participants were given a task to complete. Each one was asked to write his/her name on it using a marker pen.

Then all the balloons were collected and put in another room nearby. They were let in that room and asked to find the balloon which had their name written on it. They were given a time limit of five minutes to complete this exercise. Everyone frantically searched for their name, colliding with each other and pushing others, and there was utter chaos. At the end of five minutes, except for a few, no one could find the balloon with their name on it.

Next, the speaker modified the task slightly. This time, each one was asked to randomly collect a balloon and give it to the person whose name was written on it. Within minutes, everyone had their own balloon.

What can we learn from this story?

The moral of the story is: everyone is looking for happiness all around them, not knowing where it is. But if one becomes aware and shifts their attention to the right strategies and right factors to achieve happiness, it's within everyone's reach and way quicker than one thinks.

In our search for happiness, we are primarily looking at the external factors and believe that our happiness solely depends on them. But in reality, it's only when we redesign and rewire our brains differently, when we build happier brains, that happiness starts to surround us most of the time.

Before we begin building happier brains, let's see what a happier brain looks like.

Let's Look Inside the Happiest Brain

We all have seen happy people around us at times, though they are not plentiful these days.

How do they look? Often, they have a little smile on their faces, or sometimes a huge ear-to-ear smile; other times, they may chuckle or giggle or laugh heartily, often while playing with kids or having a great time with family and friends over dinner or drinks.

But happy, smiling faces are just output, and to only look at this output undermines the significance of internal programming that generates such kind of joyful output. There is much more going inside our brains to produce happiness that depends on our internal programming or the coding of our brain's software. Various types of chemical reactions inside our brains (more details on that later) create those feelings of joy and happiness.

When we are unaware of this internal coding, we mistakenly think that the relevant output is generated through some external factors. For example, you might think that happiness is generated solely because of having a large bank balance, luxurious house and cars, or delicious food. This is because happier faces and the external material things are both tangible. You can physically see them through your eyes and, therefore, on the surface, it appears that happiness is generated through these external factors. Yes, external factors add to happiness, but only in the short-term, and soon you look for more — they don't give you eternal happiness.

Do you want to see how does a happier brain looks on the inside?

Why not look inside the brain of a person who has been often referred to as the "happiest person in the world"?

Matthieu Ricard, a Buddhist monk with a French Ph.D. in molecular genetics and, eventually, the right-hand man for the Dalai Lama, had been the subject of intensive clinical tests at the University of Wisconsin; as a result of which he is frequently described[1] as the happiest man in the world. If you just Google "happiest person in the world" his name will pop up instantly.

---

[1] https://www.independent.co.uk/news/people/profiles/matthieu-ricard-meet-mr-happy-436652.html

The psychologist Dr. Daniel Goleman describes how a three-hour wait at an airport "sped by in minutes due to the sheer pleasure of Matthieu's orbit", as he exudes a sense of tranquility, kindness and — surprisingly enough — humor.

In 2012, as part of his research, neuroscientist Richard Davidson, a professor of psychology and psychiatry at University of Wisconsin-Madison (and reported as one of the "The 100 Most Influential People in the world" by Time Magazine) and his team wired up the monk's skull with 256 sensors and conducted hours of continuous MRI scanning as a part of research study on hundreds of advanced practitioners of meditation about the impact of meditation on human brain[2].

The scans showed that when meditating, **Ricard's brain produces a level of gamma waves** — those linked to consciousness, attention, learning and memory — 'never reported before in the neuroscience literature', as per Neuroscientist Davidson. Gamma waves are associated with the **"feeling of blessings"** and create a state of peak concentration and high levels of cognitive functioning. Neuroscientists believe that gamma waves are able to link information from all parts of the brain.

---

[2] https://www.dailymail.co.uk/health/article-2225634/Is-worlds-happiest-man-Brain-scans-reveal-French-monk-abnormally-large-capacity-joy-meditation.html

Brain scans reveal that this French monk has an 'abnormally large capacity' for joy. The scans showed excessive activity in his brain's left prefrontal cortex when compared to its right counterpart, giving him an **abnormally large capacity for happiness and a reduced propensity towards negativity.**

As you can see, the joy and happiness inside his brain didn't come from external factors; rather, it was all his inside programming through meditation and other lifestyle changes. Ricard attributes the reasons for his extreme levels of happiness to his deep meditation practices.

Practicing meditation plays a vital role in improving an individual's overall well-being. Ricard claims that after a regular practice of just one month, an individual will see benefits such as a reduction in the stress level and an increase in his/her general well-being.

But you and I don't need to turn into monks to experience an elevated level of joy. By understanding the psychology and neuroscience of happiness and implementing some simple habits, we can design a much happier brain that can empower us to experience higher dimensions and lead a quality life.

Why Do You Need a Happier Brain in Today's World?

A happier brain is a must for the overall well-being of any human being. There are huge benefits one can harness in many areas of life, be they personal, professional, relationship, etc. by understanding the psychology and neuroscience of happiness and implementing certain habits that work wonders, which we will understand in much greater detail in this book.

In his book *Happier*, Tal Ben-Shahar describes "happiness" as the ultimate currency for human life. He states, *"A human being, like a business, earns profits and suffers losses. For a human being, however, the ultimate currency is not money, nor is it any external measure, such as fame, fortune, or power. The ultimate currency for a human being is happiness."*

In fact, across all the areas of our life, happiness generates numerous positive by-products that most of us have not yet taken time to understand. When we are happier, we do not only experience more joy, contentment, love, pride, and awe, but simultaneously, we also improve other aspects of our lives: our **energy levels**, our **immune systems**, our **engagement with work** and with other people, and our **physical and mental health**. We also strengthen our feelings of **self-confidence** and **self-esteem**; we start to believe that we are worthy, develop self-compassion, and feel deserving of respect.

In becoming happier, we not only **improve the quality of our lives**, but we also share the benefits of our happiness with <u>our partners, families, communities, and even society at large.</u>

Here is a quick list of the variety of benefits developing a happier brain offers to human beings:

- Improves heart rate
- Combats stress more effectively
- Creates a stronger immune system
- Creates an overall healthier lifestyle
- Reduces pain
- Increases life longevity
- Leads to better decision-making and problem-solving
- Improves individual and team productivity
- Better customer service abilities
- Helps you to be more productive, consequently earning more

Your Happiness is in Your Hands

"Happiness is not something ready-made. It comes from your own actions."

~ Dalai Lama

Happiness is nothing but an emotional state of pleasantness, just like other emotions of fear, anger, love, etc. The ultimate desire of any human being is to be in the state of constant pleasantness, and this desire prevails from the time he/she is born on this planet. No one ever wants to go through the pain, and everyone wants to have more and more feelings of pleasure.

Tony Robbins, the world-famous motivational speaker and performance strategist, states that all our behaviors and actions are influenced by two reasons, either to avoid the pain or enhance pleasure. Whatever you do in your life, the prime motivation behind that activity can't be anything else except to reduce your pain or enhance the levels of your happiness.

One could argue that all our technological developments are solely for the reason to alleviate our pain and enhances our pleasure. Medical science and the pharmaceutical industry were established to alleviate pain. All inventions, such as aeroplane, smartphone, or televisions, were created to improve our level of comfort or give us a more entertaining life experience.

The essential point here is that **we take action only to invite more happiness** into our lives.

The quality or the direction of our actions might be flawed, and we might need some guidance, but achieving happiness is in our hands. Happiness is definitely a choice. It depends on the action or behavior we choose in our lives.

40% Rule of Happiness

Sonja Lyubomirsky, the author of *The How of Happiness,* suggests that we can significantly control the levels of our happiness based on the life values we adopt, our attitude or outlook towards the outside situation, and the habits we develop to automate certain kinds of behavior.

The "Happiness is a Stochastic Phenomenon" study, performed by David Lykken and Auke Tallegen of the University of Minnesota, shows that 50% of our happiness is dependent on our genetic makeup, and we can't change that.

Next is our life circumstances, such as education levels, marital status, wealth, etc.; these factors contribute merely an additional 10% to the level of our happiness. Money can reduce your physical pain, but it can't get you rid of your sadness. Money can definitely help you overcome all your physical discomforts and can put you in a more comfortable situation, but it can't help you get rid of mental discomfort.

The **remaining 40%** is about how you behave, act, and how you are influenced by outside circumstances. The essential thing to remember here is that 40% of the factors controlling your happiness are within your control. This means that you can start making changes in your life, without blaming the outside world or your situations. Consequently, your happiness is in your hands. You need only to choose the best possible courses of action to get yourself moving in the right direction, and that's what the objective of this book is.

But You Have to Put in the Work

Everything that matters requires some work. To achieve anything substantial in life — learn a profession, master a sport, or raise a child, for example — a great amount of effort is required. But when it comes to mastering our mental or emotional lives, we find it difficult to apply similar principles. Without effort, we might get lucky sometimes, but that's not the best way to take control of your life.

You can't rely on luck solely, be it getting success in the outside material world, or winning your mind's game. Think about how much time, efforts and commitment many people devote to physical exercise, whether it's going to the gym, jogging, kickboxing, or yoga. Similarly, if you desire greater happiness, you will need to go about it in a similar way.

To put it simply, achieving lasting happiness requires making little difficult and permanent changes that require effort and commitment every day of your life. It takes work to pursue the journey of happiness, but consider that this happiness work may be the most rewarding work you'll ever do for a richer and rewarding life. Now, are you ready to jump inside the book?

Let me give you a quick introduction to what you'll find here.

What Will You Learn From This Book

The objective of this book is to teach you how to build a happier brain. It is my humble attempt to help you work towards the sometimes elusive state of mind called happiness. First, we'll go through the most common reasons for unhappiness. Then, we will examine the psychological aspects and various theories of happiness, as well as how neuroscience plays a role in generating happiness.

Finally, we will learn about personal, professional, and relational habits designed to make life happier and more fulfilling.

I hope you enjoy reading this book, and more importantly, implement some of the positive habits you find useful.

Let's get started and learn the most common reasons that most people are not happy today.

--End of Preview—

You can read the full book here >>>
Build A Happier Brain

Other Books in Power-Up Your Brain Series

1. **Intelligent Thinking:** Overcome Thinking Errors, Learn Advanced Techniques to Think Intelligently, Make Smarter Choices, and Become the Best Version of Yourself (Power-Up Your Brain Series Book 1)

2. **Think Out of The Box:** Generate Ideas on Demand, Improve Problem Solving, Make Better Decisions, and Start Thinking Your Way to the Top (Power-Up Your Brain Series Book 2)

3. **Make Smart Choices:** Learn How to Think Clearly, Beat Information Anxiety, Improve Decision Making Skills, and Solve Problems Faster (Power-Up Your Brain Series Book 3)

4. ***Build A Happier Brain:*** *The Neuroscience and Psychology of Happiness. Learn Simple Yet Effective Habits for Happiness in Personal, Professional Life and Relationships (Power-Up Your Brain Book 4)*

5. ***Think With Full Brain:*** *Strengthen Logical Analysis, Invite Breakthrough Ideas, Level-up Interpersonal Intelligence, and Unleash Your Brain's Full Potential (Power-Up Your Brain Series Book 5)*

Copyright © 2019 by Som Bathla

All rights reserved. No part of this book may be reproduced in any form without permission in writing from the author.

No part of this publication may be reproduced or transmitted in any form or by any means, mechanical or electronic, including photocopying or recording, or by any information storage and retrieval system, or transmitted by email or by any other means whatsoever without permission in writing from the author.

Printed in Great Britain
by Amazon